T0345934

Contemplation and Kingdom

# Contemplation and Kingdom

## Aquinas Reads Richard of St. Victor

### Kevin Hart

Introduction by Cynthia R. Nielsen

St. Augustine's Press

South Bend, Indiana

Manufactured in the United States of America.

1 2 3 4 5 6   26 25 24 23 22 21 20

**Library of Congress Control Number:
2020943105**

∞ The paper used in this publication meets the mini-
mum requirements of the American National Standard
for Information Sciences – Permanence of Paper for
Printed Materials, ANSI Z39.48-1984.

St. Augustine's Press
www.staugustine.net

for Sashanna

# Introduction
## by Cynthia R. Nielsen

Kevin Hart begins his fascinating study of Richard of St. Victor with what we might call a genealogy of contemplation. He reminds us that for the ancients *theoria* was at the heart of philosophy—philosophy that, unlike today, unproblematically included religious as well as philosophical activities and *teloi*. Yet, like most important philosophical concepts, *theoria*, underwent changes and became divided. Hart turns, for instance, to Plato's and Aristotle's views of *theoria* in order to highlight how their views differed. "[F]or Plato, θεωρία (in the narrow sense) was a state to be achieved by the philosopher, which would make him resemble the gods in having sustained attention to the

Forms," and yet the philosopher was called to fulfill a second job—namely, to educate his (or her) fellow citizens.[1] (After all, Socrates' so-called "just city" permits philosopher-queens.) However, *theoria*, for Aristotle, is understood as "a private reward for the philosopher or statesman who had already worked for the πόλις, and was perhaps still working for it."[2] Christianity, of course, appropriates insights both from Plato and Aristotle while also inflecting their thought in a distinctively Christian key. Accordingly, in addition to the truth of the natural world that one can attain via the light of natural reason, we have Augustine, who develops his doctrine of divine illumination and emphasizes our need for divine grace, and Aquinas, who both affirms and has much to say about revealed truth.

As the title of his essay indicates, Hart's concern is chiefly with contemplation—in particular, "the theology of contemplation in the

1   Hart, *Contemplation and Kingdom: Aquinas Reads Richard of St. Victor*, 2.
2   Ibid.

twelfth and thirteenth centuries," and even more precisely, his concern is with "one small overlap between Richard of St. Victor (*d.* 1173) and Thomas Aquinas (1225–74)."[3] In the course of his genealogy, Hart notes that early in the history of the Latin West *theoria* is translated as *contemplatio*, and it is none other than Cicero who introduces the term in his *De natura deorum*. In Cicero's account, the term's religious and philosophical lineages remain significant. Although Cicero himself argued against, for example, auguries, he recognized their role and importance for the Republic. The auger's task was to interpret various alleged signs from the gods so that the right decision might be made regarding a military operation, or such signs might indicate whether the crops would be plentiful. Although both *theoria* and *contemplatio* have pagan inheritances, both undergo various changes when they are taken up and developed by the Christian tradition. As Hart explains, "an important shift is the Christian emphasis on μετάνοια and thereafter steady moral purification of the one who seeks

3    Ibid., 6.

to contemplate the divine."[4] Thus, to contemplate the Christian God requires both repentance and ongoing moral purification, not to mention serious study and the practice of various spiritual disciplines such as prayer and participation in the sacraments. For Augustine, in fact, contemplation is a gift—that is, a reward for the pure in heart, whose purity, of course, is never without the work of divine grace. With figures like Gregory the Great, we have an emphasis on *contemplatio* in relation to a certain allegorical approach to the Hebrew Scriptures. Christian theology and the life and activities to which it calls one are grounded "in a typical or moral reading of the Hebrew Scriptures that a literal reading of those Scriptures would not support."[5] Although contemplation might suggest a kind of peaceful tranquility, one should, Hart reminds us, keep in mind that it bears within itself a history full of "treacheries of translation" and "hermeneutical torsion."[6] Moreover, contemplation

---

4    Ibid., 10.
5    Ibid., 15.
6    Ibid., 16

involves struggle and, as Augustine regularly reminds us, requires grace. In other words, unlike the *theoria* or *contemplatio* of the Greeks and Romans, for the Christian tradition, contemplation "is not something that human beings can practice just by ourselves. One must be transformed by divine love in order to gaze upon that love."[7]

Following his genealogy of contemplation, Hart focuses his attention on Richard of St. Victor. In his treatise, *De arca mystica*, Richard "attempts to overcome the divisions in θεωρία or *contemplatio*."[8] The treatise is a tropological reading of Exod. 25:8–40, which is a passage that describes the Lord's instructions to Moses regarding how to properly construct the Ark of the Covenant. Richard's thematic interests center on natural and infused contemplation. With a view to highlighting Richard's contribution to the history of contemplation's development, Hart states that if we conceive of philosophy as "the endless task of understanding what is, how

7    Ibid.
8    Ibid.

we know it, and how we should act, we can see that his vision of contemplation integrates what would otherwise be the philosophical and the religious by way of specific approaches to phenomena and the deity and the manners in which those approaches are made."[9] As we will see, this emphasis on Richard's integrated vision of contemplation is central to Hart's account of what distinguishes Richard from St. Thomas and, one might add, what makes Richard's approach so appealing today.

In *De arca Mystica,* Richard distinguishes thinking, meditating, and contemplating. In his concise yet poetic description of each, he writes: "Thinking crawls; meditation marches and often runs; contemplation flies around everywhere and when it wishes suspends itself in the heights. Thinking is without labor and fruit; in meditation there is labor with fruit; contemplation continues without labor but with fruit. In thinking there is wandering; in meditation, investigation; in contemplation, wonder [*admiratio*].

9    Ibid., 18.

Thinking is from imagination; meditation from reason; contemplation, from understanding" [*De arca Mystica* 4.5].[10] Although Aquinas, like Aristotle, was known for his acute, analytical distinctions, Richard, too, is fond of distinctions, which is evident is his account of contemplation. For example, Richard identifies six different kinds of contemplation, and each kind, of course, has its own divisions. Richard's text also contains analyses of complex symbolism that was common in mystical treatises of that time, and Aquinas would have been both accepting of and familiar with such symbolism. Yet, according to Hart, an important difference between the two thinkers emerges—namely, for Richard, contemplation is directed at both the visible and the invisible realms and the latter includes both invisible created and uncreated entities. The significance of this point will be discussed as my essay unfolds.

As mentioned in the previous paragraph, although Aquinas was acquainted with symbolic approaches to scripture, when he

10   Ibid., 19.

discusses Richard's divisions in the *Summa Theologicae*, 2a2æ q.180 art. 4, he takes a somewhat different approach. The "pivot," as Hart puts it, "is Gregory the Great's statement in the Moralia in Job that 'In contemplation indeed it is the beginning or God that is sought [quod in contemplatione principium, quod Deus est, quaeritur].'"[11] Aquinas appeals to Gregory's claim as a justification for a division between what is primary (God) and secondary (the created order) in contemplation. Aquinas does not take issue with Richard's affirmation of both intellectual and natural entities as fitting objects of contemplation. However, given Richard's interest in and lingering upon the contemplation of the natural order in his treatise, Hart draws attention to Aquinas' opting to pass over these reflections of a "secondary" nature rather quickly.

A key claim in Hart's argument is that Aquinas could have appealed to other statements by Gregory where he discusses contemplation—after all, *Moralia in Job* contains over 1800 pages. For example, in his commentary

11    Ibid., 24.

Gregory also affirms that the goal of contemplation is neither singular nor simple but rather "should be such that it passes from the consideration [*consideranda*] of a few to the many and from the many to all things, inasmuch as it is led to move gradually, and by embracing all that is transitory it determines them and, itself nearly incomprehensible, goes on growing" [*Moralia in Job*, "Letter to Leander," 5].[12] Hart underscores this as an important difference between Aquinas and Gregory—namely, for Aquinas, contemplation is directed to the single activity of gazing upon the truth, which underlies and includes other activities, but is ultimately aimed at gazing upon God as the fitting object of our love.[13] Gregory, in contrast, as just mentioned, does not claim that contemplation has a single aim or goal. Hart provides a succinct summary of his position as follows:

> Where Gregory stresses that the aim of contemplation is inclusive,

12  Ibid., 25
13  Ibid.

Aquinas places the accent on gradual exclusion until just one pure gaze is left, and where Gregory reflects on natural phenomena [,] Aquinas has in mind the grasping of intellectual principles. Later in the same commentary, Gregory observes that David contemplated his moral condition and Paul his weakness; and for Aquinas these acts would not be contemplation as such but rather exercises of the moral virtues, which will dispose one to gaze upon the deity. [...] Had Aquinas chosen the passage about the need to contemplate the many from the *Moralia* for the *sed contra* to 2a2ae q. 180 art. 4 we might have acquired a more generous account of Richard's vision of contemplation, one that does not consign attention to the natural world to secondary concerns.[14]

14   Ibid., 26–27.

This last sentence is the crux of the matter, as it underscores how Aquinas' selective reading of Gregory colors his reading of Richard and, as Hart puts it, relegates "attention to the natural world to secondary concerns."[15]

Of course, for Richard and other premodern Christian thinkers, Scripture specifies "how being is articulated" and reveals truths about reality that surpass natural reason.[16] Even so, one might wonder whether Richard's proliferation of modes and divisions are examples of constructing rather than drawing distinctions or of imagining rather than disclosing phenomena. However one decides, Hart's analysis makes a strong case for further investigating the differences between Richard and St. Thomas on contemplation. The significance of these differences and their consequences, at this point in the essay, remains unclarified. Before taking a step in that direction, Hart says that first we need to answer the following question: Is Richard's understanding of contemplation

15   Ibid., 27.
16   Ibid., 32.

the same as Aquinas'? In other words, are we even dealing with the same concept of contemplation or perhaps is an equivocation at work?

As we observed earlier, for Aquinas, "contemplation is limited to God as the proper object of our love," which, as Hart states, is "a mild criticism of Richard."[17] In line with Aquinas' criticism, Dante presents Richard in the tenth canto of the *Paradiso* not "as a contemplative but as an advocate and practioner of *consideratione*."[18] Richard, in fact, often employs the word *consideratione*, describing it as that which "prepares us for *contemplatio* and even overlaps with it a little."[19] Given Aquinas' emphasis on contemplation as ascent, he selectively tracks Richard's metaphors that signal verticality— for example, the wings and ladder of contemplation and "the watchtower of understanding."[20] However, the metaphor

17  Ibid., 34.
18  Ibid.
19  Ibid., 37.
20  Ibid., 38.

that signals the horizontal—St. Paul's mirror of contemplation found in 1 Cor. 13:12—is categorized as an act of meditation rather than contemplation.[21] Although it is clear from Richard's commentary on Exod. 25:8–40, that he, too, cherishes ascent, it is, nonetheless, significant that he includes this metaphor of the horizontal. Hart ends this section with a rather interesting, albeit speculative, possibility: Might we, perhaps, read Richard's allegory of the ark of the covenant not only vertically but also horizontally? And if so, would this grant a repose "in the ascent in order to contemplate the good things that God has created in the natural world and for the exercise of the intellect"? In short, Hart asks: Does "contemplation include the Kingdom as well as the King?"[22]

Hart emphasizes how, for Richard, nothing is in principle excluded from the activity of contemplation. In other words, not only is contemplation focused on God's creative deeds as well as his being and attributes, but

21   Ibid., 39.
22   Ibid., 40.

also Richard's extensive view of contemplation extends to the created order and our intellectual engagement with it. Even though
he presents us with a hierarchy moving from
thinking, to meditating, to contemplating, he
also affirms that "there is nothing excluded
from contemplation. No change of object is
required, only a shift of attitude. One passes
from regarding and examining to marveling,
all of which presumes the disciplined
monastic life that is taught in the Abbey."[23]

Since later in the paper Hart highlights
connections between Richard of St. Victor
and twentieth-century philosopher Edmund
Husserl, I want to gesture toward areas of
convergence with a few other contemporary
Continental figures. For example, the contemplative activity and attunement that Hart
describes in this section of his essay sounds
similar to certain emphases in the hermeneutical tradition. Here I am thinking primarily
of Martin Heidegger and Hans-Georg
Gadamer, both of whom underscore the
need for a special kind of comportment, for

23   Ibid., 46.

instance, toward a work of art; however, this attuned engagement could also apply to a natural entity such as the leaf Hart mentions. In his post-*Truth and Method* writings on art, Gadamer, influenced by Heidegger, often employs the term *verweilen,* which can be translated as "to linger, tarry, or dwell with something." *Verweilen* or tarrying refers to the spectator's or auditor's comportment (*Haltung*) toward an artwork. This engaged, attuned comportment underscores one aspect of the temporal dimension of our experience (*Erfahrung*) of art. First, the engaged participant must spend time or linger with the artwork, since it takes time for the various facets of an artwork to unfold. Moreover, one must linger with it on more than one occasion; great art is neither an object of consumption nor does it disclose its insights and truths "on demand." Second, the artwork itself has its own rhythm or unique temporal unfolding, which Gadamer calls the artwork's *Weile.* (Literally, *die Weile* means "while" or "moment.") When one lingers with an artwork and allows it "to come forth," one enters into what Gadamer refers to as "festival" or "fulfilled time" which contrasts with "empty time." Empty time is characteristic of our daily life; that is, we oscillate from being frenzied or not having enough time to complete our tasks, to being bored or having too much time. In this regard, time is measured and quantified, and we regard time as something we fill, waste, or even control. Empty time is perceived as a succession of moments—moments that arrive from the future and vanish into the past. Yet in our daily tasks we experience empty time as primarily future-oriented. We are concerned, for instance, with how to accomplish our career goals, how to arrange our schedule or family life in order to have enough time to complete our dissertation or book, or how to fill our time during a holiday break. Here present time is intimately related to our anticipation of future time and thus becomes "time for" completing this or that task or "time until" our next vacation or sabbatical. Festival or fulfilled time is experienced quite differently. In festival time, a rupture occurs in linear time and, as it were, a "space" opens for the while (*die Weile*) of the artwork. Here time is not measured, but rather every moment of the artwork's unfolding is fulfilled, or we might say with a nod to Jean-Luc Marion, saturated. Importantly, for Gadamer, festival time does not transport the spectator or auditor into another world—a world without time—but is rather a transcendence within immanence; that is, in lingering with the artwork, one is so drawn in and absorbed in the movement of the artwork that one's normal experience of time is transcended. I am curious as to whether Richard's discussion of contemplation includes any reflections on time or temporality that might share similarities with the Gadamerian or Heideggerian hermeneutical tradition. If so, I hope that Hart's present or future research on Richard will explore these connections.

Having retraced Hart's argument and gestured toward connections with the hermeneutic tradition, I now turn to somewhat critical remarks. Hart states that on Richard's view, moving "from regarding and examining to marveling" presupposes "the disciplined monastic life that is taught in the

Abbey."[24] Yet, as Hart unfolds Richard's position, it is not clear why the habits needed for contemplation could not also be attained outside the Abbey. In other words, a philosophically trained, virtuous Christian could also contemplatively engage and marvel at the natural world, a work of art, other human beings, and intellectual principles and intelligible structures. Moreover, I do not see why one couldn't make similar claims with respect to disciplined, virtuous (and even those who were not so virtuous) non-believing philosophers? Consider Plato, Aristotle, Heidegger (with his clearly unvirtuous commitments to National Socialism and support of Hitler), Gadamer, and the list goes on. If non-believing philosophers are excluded, what is the basis of this exclusion? Is it because their contemplative activities do not have their *telos* in God? If so, then how is Richard's position *essentially* different from Aquinas'? Would we not instead have a difference of emphasis? And perhaps a difference of emphasis is all that Hart claims;

24   Ibid.

however, statements like this one regarding the need for a monastic life of discipline and, as discussed in the following paragraph, that "one must prepare to contemplate anything by exercising the virtues"[25] seem to undermine Hart's argument. Such claims, as well as those regarding the prerequisite of living a disciplined monastic life, require more elaboration. Later, I shall suggest that even if what we have is a difference of emphasis, such a difference, over time, can prove significant in practical matters, especially when it comes to how we see and interact with the natural world and other human individuals and cultures which whom we differ.

After having again reiterated the need, on Richard's view, to prepare for contemplation through "exercising the virtues," Hart says that "Richard excludes nothing in principle from contemplation" and that those familiar with and shaped by "the tradition that comes to us from Shaftesbury, Kant and Schopenhauer" will find this somewhat surprising and even objectionable. Since Hart

25  Ibid.

mentions Kant in his list, I would like to suggest another way of presenting a Kantian response that problematizes Hart's claims. My appeal to Kant should not be taken as a wholesale endorsement of every aspect of his position; rather, Kant's aesthetics and his account of how aesthetic contemplation of nature and our experience of the sublime have ties to morality, freedom, and our recognition of ourselves as spiritual and moral beings, serve as a challenge to what Hart's presentation of Richard's seemingly Christian-exclusive access to contemplation—that is, contemplation that has the potential to transform one's way of seeing the (natural and social world) and one's relationship to the (natural) world and other human beings.

By way of review, in the *Critique of Judgment,* Kant distinguishes between the pleasure and satisfaction one finds in the agreeable, the good, and the beautiful.[26] For present purposes, I will focus on the agreeable and the beautiful. In his discussion of

26  See, for example, Kant, *Critique of Judgment,* §§3–5.

our pleasure in the agreeable, which involves the gratification we experience when (in moderation) we satisfy our hunger, thirst, or other bodily desires, Kant's point is that the pleasure that comes from this type of satisfaction is different in kind than the satisfaction we experience in the beautiful. Moreover, the latter does not involve consuming the object, treating it as a means to another end, or using it for some practical or useful purpose. Satisfaction in the beautiful occurs when we engage an object via aesthetic contemplation and experience disinterested pleasure as a result of the free play of our imagination and understanding.

In the third *Critique*, Kant is, of course, most concerned with natural beauty, although the free play of our cognitive faculties and the accompanying disinterested pleasure also apply, as he acknowledges, to our contemplation of artworks. While Kant does not, as Richard does, emphasize a need for divine grace to contemplate natural beauty, beautiful works of art, or the sublime, he does connect such contemplation to our moral and spiritual nature. For example, in his discussion of the sublime, Kant states that we first have an experience of displeasure because our imagination is overwhelmed and cannot handle the immensity of the experience. However, the initial displeasure facilitates the realization that we are supersensible creatures that exceed both the magnitude of the quantitative or mathematical sublime and the power or might of the qualitative or dynamic sublime. As Kant puts it in §27 of the *Critique of Judgment*, "the inner perception of the inadequacy of every standard of sense to serve for the rational estimation of magnitude is a coming into accord with reason's laws, and a displeasure that arouses the feeling of our own supersensible vocation, according to which it is purposive, and consequently a pleasure, to find every standard of sensibility falling short of the ideas of reason."[27] Thus, through this initial experience of displeasure we come to see that there is something in us greater than nature (i.e., freedom and morality), which implies that our final end transcends (causally

27   Kant, *Critique of Judgment*, 88; 5:258; §27.

determined) nature. For Kant, in the experience of the sublime we discover that we are not only rational but spiritual and moral beings endowed with purpose separate from and transcending that of nature.[28]

Later, in §42 Kant connects one's "*immediate interest* in the beauty of *nature* (not merely to have taste in judging it)" as an indication that one possesses a "good soul."[29] That is, when one contemplates the beautiful forms of nature and takes an immediate, intellectual (rather than empirical) interest in their beauty, one is drawn to them not for utility-value or other benefits that they might yield. In fact, one of Kant's main concerns in §42 is to highlight similarities between natural beauty and morality.[30] As he explains, when

28  See, for example, Kant, *Critique of Judgment,* §§27–29.
29  Kant, *Critique of Judgment,* 128; 5:299; §42.
30  Although I will not discuss his justification for his claims regarding natural beauty and morality, one can find Kant's explanations as to why we tend to make connections with beauty and morality in §59 in his discussion of beauty as a symbol of morality.

we contemplate nature's beauty, we come to see an artfulness in nature. He even goes so far as to say that when we contemplate the beautiful in nature, it is *as if* the language of nature were addressing us and pointing us to "a higher meaning."[31] Moreover, nature's beauty is perceived as possessing a "purposiveness apart from any purpose," and, consequently, seems to be given *for us*—that is, it seems to be given to us for our sheer (aesthetic) delight.[32] In short, that nature displays a purposiveness without purpose, to which we are drawn and in which we find pleasure, awakens us to our moral calling and our status as free, moral beings.

Given what I have sketched above in reference to Kant, I find Hart's claim that "we will be pressed to distinguish aesthetic contemplation from its religious counterpart. What is intolerable for the former is possible for the latter because of moral discipline and

---

31  Kant, *Critique of Judgment,* 131; 5:302; §42. Kant gives the example of a bird's song expressing its "joyousness and contentment with its existence."

32  Kant, *Critique of Judgment,* 130; 5:301; §42.

Grace," unconvincing.[33] At the very least, the tradition from Shaftesbury, Kant, and Schopenhauer is more complicated and robust than Hart's description implies, and Kant's aesthetics, in particular, call into question the claims that Hart vis-à-vis Richard makes about the need for grace and monastic discipline as a propaedeutic for contemplative activity—and especially so in light of his argument stressing the differences between Richard and Aquinas. Although Kant's position suggests a connection between aesthetic contemplation and morality (which is not to say that this is an uncontested point among Kant and other scholars), he makes no appeals to the need for divine grace. Moreover, what he describes seems to allow for the possibility that our contemplation of natural beauty can expand and deepen our moral understanding and give rise to something like a religious experience (broadly construed) or at least a spiritual awakening.

In addition, when it comes to thinkers in the hermeneutical tradition such as

33  Hart, *Contemplation and Kingdom*, 48.

Gadamer and Heidegger, who, although influenced by Kantian aesthetics, drop Kant's particular way of connecting beauty and morality, there are fruitful connections worth exploring. For example, the contemplative activity and attunement that Hart describes in his discussion of Richard of St. Victor resonates with certain emphases in both Heidegger and Gadamer. As mentioned earlier, both thinkers underscore the need for a special kind of comportment—namely, "tarrying" or "lingering" (*verweilen*)—when engaging a work of art. This attuned tarrying could also apply to a natural entity or a mundane object such a bridge or a clay jug. Moreover, in line with Richard's thought, for the philosophical hermeneut, lingering with Dutch vanitas still-life paintings in which a not-so-beautiful human skull is prominently featured might yield significant insights regarding life's fleetingness and might even facilitate a transformative event. For the hermeneut, the artwork or other with which we linger need not be beautiful; rather, what is required is a proper attunement and openness to what the other might disclose and a willingness to learn and be changed. Such disclosures could involve the kinds of insights that Richard describes such as a deeper grasp of our moral inadequacy and finitude, our need for others for proper self-understanding, and our wonder that there is something rather than nothing. In fact, the diverse modes, which include *dilatio mentis* or "an enlarging of the mind," *sublevatio mentis* or "a raising of the mind" that increase one's knowledge, and *excessus mentis* or "the overflowing of the mind, or ecstasy" all find analogous correlates in the hermeneutical tradition especially in its Gadamerian and Heideggerian expressions.[34]

34  Hart, *Contemplation and Kingdom*, 60. It even seems possible to include the three moments of the third mode (*excessus mentis*) in an account of hermeneutical aesthetic contemplation, although Richard's notion of *magnitudo devotionis* or "greatness of devotion" and the desire to be "taken out of the body and to be one with God" would be rejected by many or revised to include embodied experiences of immanent or this-

Returning to Hart's analysis of the differences between Richard and St. Thomas, Hart states that although Aquinas supports the "mixed life," his "strict separation of the active and contemplative lives" moves him away from affirming the modes that Richard articulates.[35] Furthermore, Richard's modes are porous and blur the boundaries between the active and contemplative life. One engaged in the active life, for example, can likewise contemplate and experience an enlarging or raising of the mind. Underscoring this difference between the Angelic Doctor and Richard of St. Victor, Hart writes:

> Unrestricted to particular levels of ascent, which Aquinas notionally assigns only to those in the contemplative state of life, the modes can be freely used in the world or in the cloister. [...] One question to keep

worldly transcendence. For an example of how one might connect Richard's modes to Gadamer's hermeneutical aesthetics, see Gadamer, "The Artwork in Word and Image."
35    Ibid., 20.

in mind as we continue is whether Aquinas quietly assimilates the human order, physical and moral, to the natural order when he consigns the natural order to secondary status with respect to divine ascent and, if he does, to what extent he does so, even when he affirms the value of the mixed life."[36]

In the remainder of this section, Hart focuses on the attractiveness of Richard's position—namely, that it calls us to open ourselves "to God by attending to the created order around us. [...] Another part of the allure is that in allowing ourselves to approach God through wonder in creation we do not abandon our bodily selves but see there an excellence in having been created in that way. Yet we also long for self-transcendence, not merely evacuation of the self."[37]

Richard's emphasis on the created order and its rich contemplative possibilities is, to

36  Ibid., 63–64.
37  Ibid., 65.

be sure, appealing and especially so in our current environmental crisis. In mid-January we watched in horror as part of Australia was swallowed in flames resulting in the destruction of over 46 million acres of land and more than a billion native animals, as well as the loss of at least 29 human lives (as of Jan. 17, 2020).[38] One wonders what it will take for us to see the beauty and mystery of the created order and then to individually and collectively take meaningful action through legislative and lifestyle changes to respect, preserve, and nurture it as the stewards of the earth that we are called to be. Can one truly love the Creator and be unmoved and inactive when creation so intensely "groans"—to borrow a metaphor from St. Paul's epistle to the Romans?

In the paragraphs that follow, I revisit the topic of our present environmental crisis and

38   Dana Nuccitelli. "How Climate Change Influenced Australia's Unprecedented Fires." *Yale Climate Connections.* January 17, 2020. https://www.yaleclimateconnections.org/2020/01/how-climate-change-influenced-australias-unprecedented-fires/ (Accessed January 23, 2020.)

how contemplative lingering with and attunement to the earth's beauty and its groaning is one step toward responding to our mandate to be good stewards of the gift we have received. In addition, I gesture toward how Richard's emphases on contemplation and the natural world are relevant to two pressing contemporary issues—namely, the environmental crisis and the question: Who is our neighbor?

First, let us turn to Hart's fascinating discussion of Richard and Edmund Husserl, wherein Richard's *De arca mystica* can be understood as a proto-phenomenological text. Hart observes that Richard's allegory in *De arca mystica* "is also a coded naming of something like, what centuries later, Husserl would call the 'regions of being' [...] For Husserl, these 'regions' are not spatial areas but the highest generic unities that belong to an individual whole, each of which has a unique regional ontology that offers an eidetic science appropriate to it."[39] Richard had his own version of something akin to

39  Hart, *Contemplation and Kingdom*, 71–72.

Husserl's "regions of being"; however, the key difference between the two is that Richard's "regional ontology" includes the divine and Husserl's does not.[40] Another important difference is that Husserl's understanding of *theoria* requires us to bracket or suspend presuppositions and interests, whereas Richard's contemplative activity would find such a requirement unreasonable. Summarizing this point, Hart writes: "The philosopher seeks knowledge without presuppositions; the Christian must always lovingly presuppose a creating and redeeming God. To which we might add: The philosopher begins in wonder and hopes to end in understanding, while the person contemplating God begins in wonder and is moved to greater wonder (*magnitudo admirationis*)."[41] Granted, Hart's main contemporary dialogue partner is Husserl and, by and large, I agree with his assessment of Husserl on this point; however, what he describes fails to adequately characterize some of Husserl's most

40   Ibid., 74.
41   Ibid., 81.

important philosophical "offspring"— namely, Heidegger and Gadamer, both of whom emphasize the role of fore-conceptions and prejudgments in our interpretative endeavors. Moreover, Heidegger, Gadamer, and other contemporary philosophers endorse the notion of philosophy beginning in wonder and moving to greater wonder. So here again, it seems that there are interesting and fruitful overlaps between Richard and contemporary Continental philosophers worthy of further investigation.

In his discussion of Richard and Husserl, Hart points out that both were drawn to and influenced by Augustine's text "*De vera religione*." In particular, they were drawn to the notion that truth is found in the "inner man," yet they appropriated the concept differently. Whereas Husserl "took the 'inner man' to be transcendental, Richard, like Augustine sought an inner man who was created in order to transcend the world, a man whose soul was formed so that it would bear the *imago dei* and finally be one with God."[42] Of

42  Ibid., 71.

course, as Hart is at pains to stress, this call to "transcend the world" is not, for Richard, a call to negate, disparage, or neglect the created order. I imagine that a Thomist would rather quickly want to interject that this description of Richard likewise fits St. Thomas. He, too, affirms the goodness of the created order. Hence, the Thomist might ask whether the differences that Hart highlights between Richard and St. Thomas are more differences of emphasis than essential differences. Even if we grant that what we have are differing emphases, might it be the case that their, as it were, effective history (*Wirkungsgeschichte*) accumulates over time into something more substantive through translation into the practical realm of lived experience? That is, if contemplation has only God as its object, and the natural order is seen *merely* as a means to God, does it make it easier for communities and individuals of faith to justify neglecting, for example, our mandate to care for the earth and the entirety of the earthly created order, which includes *not only humans*, but non-human animals and ecosystems? In other words, while it is certainly the case that St. Thomas himself upholds the goodness of the created order, perhaps *we* have come to see the created world primarily as something to master, dominate, and even, exploit for profit.

In his encyclical, *Laudato Si': On Care For Our Common Home,* Pope Francis indicates that since the early 70s, starting with Pope Paul the VI's Apostolic Letter *Octogesima Adveniens* and reiterated in the writings of every subsequent pope up to the present day, there is a growing concern that we as a human society have come to see the natural world as simply a means for our consumption and exploitation. It is well known that Pope Francis has been perhaps the most outspoken Pope on environmental issues, having devoted significant space to the topic in *Laudato Si'*. However, as Francis points out, in (now saint) John Paul II's first encyclical, *Redemptor Hominis*, he, too, expresses concern that humans seem "to see no other meaning in their natural environment than what serves for immediate use and consumption."[43] In

43   *Laudato Si'*, paragraph 5. The quote from John

his *Catechesis* delivered on January 17, 2001, John Paul II uses even *stronger* words and issues a more *severe* warning, suggesting that humans have continued on the same path of domination and destruction instead of stewardship and nurture. For example, he writes in paragraphs 3 and 4:

> Unfortunately, if we scan the regions of our planet, we immediately see that humanity has disappointed God's expectations. Man, especially in our time, has without hesitation devastated wooded plains and valleys, polluted waters, disfigured the earth's habitat, made the air unbreathable, disturbed the hydrogeological and atmospheric systems, turned luxuriant areas into deserts and undertaken forms of unrestrained industrialization, degrading that "flowerbed"—to

Paul II is taken from his Encyclical Letter *Redemptor Hominis* (4 March 1979), 15: *AAS* 71 (1979), 287.

use an image from Dante (Paradiso, XXII, 151)—which is the earth, our dwelling-place.

We must therefore encourage and support the "ecological conversion" which in recent decades has made humanity more sensitive to the catastrophe to which it has been heading. Man is no longer the Creator's "steward," but an autonomous despot, who is finally beginning to understand that he must stop at the edge of the abyss.[44]

Both John Paul II and Pope Francis, in a way that Richard would approve, do not rigidly separate the gift, wonder, and beauty of human life from the gift, wonder, and beauty of the natural world, and this includes even the intricacies and innerworkings of the

44 John Paul II, *Catechesis* (17 January 2001), paragraphs 3 and 4. http://www.vatican.va/content/john-paul-ii/en/audiences/2001/documents/hf_jp-ii_aud_20010117.html. Accessed January 13, 2020.

biotic and abiotic components of our ecological systems.

A final point that I would like to discuss is Hart's emphasis on Richard's integrated view of love of God and love of neighbor. Hart states that, for Richard, God gives himself to us in and through love—both his love freely given and our love for Him birthed and nurtured through grace. Since love of God and love of neighbor are so closely intertwined in scripture, Hart asks whether God's love is also disclosed through love of neighbor. The Christian, as Hart observes, is called to a special kind of love—namely, *agape,* which is the highest expression of love and is not offered based on the other's moral, social, political, or religious standing. Hart then draws our attention to a very important linguistic point in the Greek text of St. Luke's account of the Good Samaritan. For example, Hart writes: "'Neighbor' [πλησίον] needs to be distinguished from 'brother' [ἀδελφός] or 'sister' [ἀδελφή]. In the radical sense that Jesus gives to the word, exemplified most sharply in the parable of the Good Samaritan (Luke 10: 25–37), the neighbor is the person who breaches the horizon of one's world with a call for help to alleviate his material or spiritual poverty."[45]

*Plesion* [πλησίον] is also the word used in St. Mark's iteration of the Great Commandment where we are instructed to love God with everything that we are and to love our neighbor [πλησίον] as ourselves (Mark 12:30–31). Importantly, the neighbor is not limited to one's Christian brother or sister or one's family members. As New Testament scholar N. T. Wright reminds us, Samaritans and Jews had been enemies for centuries as "both sides claimed to be the true inheritors of the promises to Abraham and Moses."[46] Wright also comments on the opening exchange between Jesus and the lawyer, whose aim was to test Jesus. The lawyer, Wright explains,

> wants to know who counts as 'neighbour.' For him, God is the God of Israel, and neighbours are Jewish neighbours. For Jesus (and

45   Hart, *Contemplation and the Kingdom*, 86.
46   Wright, *Luke for Everyone*, 127.

for Luke, who highlights this theme), Israel's God is the God of grace for the whole world, and a neighbour is anybody in need. Jesus' telling question at the end isn't asking who the Samaritan regarded as his neighbour. He asked, instead, who *turned out to be* the neighbour of the half-dead Jew lying in the road. Underneath the apparently straightforward moral lesson […], we find a much sterner challenge exactly fitting in with the emphasis of Luke's story so far. Can you recognize the hated Samaritan as your neighbour?[47]

Or perhaps to bring the question closer to home: Can we recognize the immigrant as *our* neighbor, or the child separated from her parents at the border as *our* neighbors? And, importantly, can we be a neighbor to them? If we attend to the parable, we notice that the Samaritan does not help the injured man

---

47   Ibid., 127–28.

because of the his social, political, or religious status or because he was regarded as morally virtuous. Rather, he helps an "enemy" and at cost to himself. To employ Hart's words, the Samaritan loves the King through the Kingdom. In short, Richard's "Kingdom attitude" involves overcoming "any artificial division between the King and the Kingdom, any undue spiritualization of the Kingdom, as well as the distinction between the primary and the secondary, as Aquinas formulates it with respect to the contemplative life."[48] I will leave it to the Thomists to decide whether St. Thomas himself over-spiritualizes the Kingdom; but no matter how that debate plays out, Hart's reflections on Richard are inspiring, intellectually stimulating, not to mention individually and collectively challenging and relevant to our twenty-first-century context. With pressing sociopolitical issues such as our environmental crisis and now a global pandemic (Covid-19), thinking through our relation to the natural world, non-human animals, and

48   Hart, *Contemplation and the Kingdom*, 118.

human others is no longer something that we can delay; it presses upon us with an existential urgency that we ignore to our own peril. An attunement and comportment of genuine care, nurture, respect, wonder, and love, as Richard would put it, for the created order *is* our calling. Perhaps a combination of Richard's contemplative approach and the hermeneutic tradition's attentive lingering can help to reshape how we see our interconnectedness with the natural world, non-human animals, and other human beings. Strangely, something invisible to the naked eye—a virus—has revealed and made present in a powerful, even visceral way our interconnectedness, interdependence, fragility, and vulnerability; it has likewise made evident—if we have eyes to see—how damaging and disease-inducing our current practices such as factory farming are to the earth and all natural others, humans included.[49] Given the ever-present presence of

49   See, for example, David Benatar, "Our Cruel Treatment of Animals Led to the Coronavirus." *New York Times.* April 13, 2020. https://www.

the virus—whether in the daily reporting of confirmed cases and deaths or in our anxieties for our own well-being and that of our family and friends—our shelter-in-place, social distancing scenario affords us the opportunity to reflect upon how we *are* in and with the natural world and our neighbors. Perhaps the sound of birdsong, no longer drowned out by cars, planes, and the like will catch our ears, arrest our attention, and

nytimes.com/2020/04/13/opinion/animal-cruelty-coronavirus.html?smid=fb-share&fb-clid=IwAR3vZTltDdRp9RxBQb3QLsUwnJCHl w9wWhPUSDqJ7nrLVoFezXqbB4fGgDE. Accessed April 14, 2020. Benatar contends that Covid-19 as a zoonotic disease is an outcome of intentional human practices. In the case of Covid-19 animals, he points to China's "wet markets," where animals are housed in cruel, unsanitary conditions which easily facilitate the transmission of diseases from animals to animal as well as animal to humans. Of course, the U.S. is replete with factory farms in which similar cruel practices and unsanitary conditions abound. The problem, in other words, is a *human* problem. For Americans to place the blame on China is the height of hypocrisy and neglects our own moral failings in this realm.

}xlix{

move us to linger with its sonorous beauty. And perhaps in this unprecedented moment, our attunement to the birdsong's singular melody will facilitate contemplative reflection that will transform how we see ourselves in relation to earth and natural others and thus motivate us to live in a more harmonious relationship with the earth and natural others. If so, *mutatis mutandis* we will foster and advance an integrated contemplative life, and one of which I imagine Richard would applaud.

# Bibliography

Benatar, David. "Our Cruel Treatment of Animals Led to the Coronavirus." *New York Times*. April 13, 2020. https://www.nytimes.com/2020/04/13/opinion/animal-cruelty-coronavirus.html?smid=fb-share&fbclid=IwAR3vZTltDdRp9RxBQ b3QLsUwnJCHlw9wWhPUSDqJ7nrLVo FezXqbB4fGgDE. Accessed April 14, 2020.

Gadamer, Hans-Georg. "The Artwork in Work and Image: 'So True, So Full of Being!'" In *The Gadamer Reader: A Bouquet of Later Writings*, edited by Richard E. Palmer, 192–224. Evanston, IL: Northwestern University Press, 2007.

Kant, Immanuel. *Critique of Judgment*. Translated by James Creed Meredith. Revised, edited and introduced by Nicholas Walker. Oxford: Oxford University Press, 2008.

Nuccitelli, Dana. "How Climate Change Influenced Australia's Unprecedented Fires." *Yale Climate Connections.* January 17, 2020. https://www.yaleclimateconnections.org/2020/01/how-climate-change-influenced-australias-unprecedented-fires/. Accessed January 23, 2020.

Pope Francis. *Laudato Si': On Care for Our Common Home.* http://www.vatican.va/content/francesco/en/encyclicals/documents/papa-francesco_20150524_enciclica-laudato-si.html. Accessed January 13, 2020.

John Paul II, *Catechesis* (17 January 2001), paragraphs 3 and 4. http://www.vatican.va/content/john-paul-ii/en/audiences/2001/documents/hf_jp-ii_aud_20010117.html. Accessed January 13, 2020.

Wright, N. T. *Luke for Everyone,* 2nd edition. Westminster: John Knox Press, 2004.

# CONTEMPLATION AND KINGDOM:
## AQUINAS READS RICHARD OF ST. VICTOR

The word "contemplation" comes to us with a divided history, not once but several times. As a placing shot, we might say that the primary division is between philosophy and religion, but in saying so we should be cautioned that this distinction is quite late and unstable. For θεωρία was widely regarded in the ancient world as central to the exercise of φιλοσοφία, which has ends we would identify today as both philosophical and religious; and these impinge on us even before we distinguish a pre-philosophical commitment to religion in the activities of the θεωροί, private and public, who traveled to witness the spectacle of religious festivals.[1] And θεωρία itself was divided and became so again. First, the word is used in a broad sense ("observation") and in a narrow sense ("contemplation").[2] Second, for Plato, θεωρία (in the narrow sense) was a state to be achieved by the philosopher, which would make him resemble the gods in having sustained attention to the Forms, but it was not a condition to which one should cling single-mindedly, for one also had a responsibility to educate the πόλις.[3] Yet, for Aristotle, θεωρία (in the same narrow sense) was a private reward for the philosopher or statesman who had already worked for the πόλις, and was perhaps still working for it, whether in teaching metaphysics and ethics, and investigating

---

1    See, on this theme, Andrea Wilson Nightingale, *Spectacles of Truth in Classical Greek Philosophy: "Theoria" in its Cultural Context* (Cambridge: Cambridge University Press, 2004).

2    For a discussion of the two senses, see David Roochnik, "What is *Theoria*?: *Nichomachean Ethics*, Book 10.7-8," *Classical Philology*, 104: 1 (2009), 69-82.

3    See Plato, *Republic*, 517d and *Phaedrus*, 247b-c.

nature, or examining constitutions, reflecting on political responsibilities and crafting legislation.[4]

Christianity is heir to both sides of the division between the two generative ancient philosophers while redirecting the thought of both so as to be centered on truth that has been illumined by God (Augustine) or that has been revealed by God (Aquinas), not just the truth that phenomena disclose. The division and centering give rise to what, in an augmented tradition that gains strength and focus with Gregory the Great's *Liber regulæ pastoralis* (*c.* 590), we call the "mixed life"; and it equally brings about what, with the Desert Fathers and, later, those who followed the *Regula Sancti Benedicti*, such as the Benedictines and the Cistercians, we call the "contemplative life."[5]

4    See Plato, *Republic*, books 5-7, and Aristotle, *Nicomachean Ethics*, ch. 10.

5    See Gregory the Great, *Book of Pastoral Rule*, trans. George Demacopoulos (Crestwood, NY: St. Vladimir Seminary Press, 2007), Part 1.5 and Part 2, and also *Moral Reflections on the Book of Job*, 6 vols, trans. Brian Kerns, intro. Mark DelCogliano (Collegeville: Liturgical Press,

The one leans towards obligation, the other to reward. To be sure, Christianity also inherits from other Greek philosophical schools, notably the Stoics, who advocated diverse meditative exercises to help us cope with an uncertain life that certainly ends in death; but meditation in its sundry transformations, particularly what became known as *consideratione*, will remain a little to the side here. My focus will be contemplation. Its philosophical heritage is readily apparent in our ordinary linguistic acts, as when we speak of contemplating problems, situations and places. But I will say little or nothing about those acts. Nor will I say much about how, in a

2014-20), 6.37.56, 59. Before Gregory the "mixed life" was a theme explored by Gregory Nazianzen in his "Apology for his Flight to Pontus" (Oration 2), *Nicene and Post-Nicene Fathers: Second Series*, ed. Philip Schaff et al., 7 (1885; rpt. Peabody, MA: Hendrickson, 1996), 204-27, and by John Cassian in his *Conferences*, trans. Colm Luibheid (New York: Paulist Press, 1985), conference 18. After them, an important short text on the subject was composed by Walter Hilton (*c*. 1342-96), *Mixed Life*, trans. Rosemary Dorward, intro. and notes John Clark (Oxford: SLG Press, 2001).

far more specialized way, some modern
philosophers, most notably Husserl and
Wittgenstein, sometimes regard their practice
as contemplative.[6] Nonetheless, I will bring

6   See Ludwig Wittgenstein, *Culture and Value*, ed.
    G. H. von Wright in collaboration with Heikki
    Nyman, trans. Peter Winch (Chicago: Univer-
    sity of Chicago Press, 1984), 2e. In his early
    work Wittgenstein regards philosophy as essen-
    tially concerned with clarification, an impulse
    that continues, in one way or another, through-
    out his work. "Philosophy is not a theory but an
    activity" he says in the *Tractatus Logico-Philo-
    sophicus*, intro. Bertrand Russell (London:
    Kegan Paul, Trench, Trubner and Co., 1922),
    4.112. "Activity" here does not rub up against
    "contemplation" as it does in much theology of
    contemplation, however. Also see D. Z. Phillips,
    *Philosophy's Cool Place* (Ithaca: Cornell Univer-
    sity Press, 1999) and *Religion and the Hermeneu-
    tics of Contemplation* (Cambridge: Cambridge
    University Press, 2001). For Husserl on philos-
    ophy as contemplative, see Lev Shestov's con-
    versation with him as reported in his "In
    Memory of a Great Philosopher: Edmund
    Husserl," trans. George Kline, *Speculation and
    Revelation*, trans. Bernard Martin (Athens: Ohio
    University Press, 1982), 272. The relevant sen-
    tence is *"Philosophie ist Besinnung,"* where *Besin-*

Husserl into the conversation a bit later, for there are hidden paths that link him to my principal concerns. In the main, though, I will restrict myself to the theology of contemplation in the twelfth and thirteenth centuries, and even there to just one small overlap between Richard of St. Victor (*d.* 1173) and Thomas Aquinas (1225-74).[7] Both were nourished by a Latin

*nung* means reflection, contemplation or meditation. Also see Stephan Strasser, "Erfahrung und Kontemplation," *Welt im Widerspruch: Gedanken zu einer Phänomenologie als ethischer Fundamentalphilosophie* (Dordrecht: Kluwer, 1991), 49-51.

7  Aquinas also mentions Richard of St. Victor in many places, though not as often as one finds in Bonaventure. The *Index Thomisticus* gives fourteen citations in the commentary on the *Sententiæ*, four in the *Summa theologiæ*, two in *De veritate*, fourteen in *De potentia dei*, and more in other works. There is little commentary on the relation. See, however, Emmanuel Durand, "Comment practiquer la théologie trinitaire en pèlerin? Béatitude et trinité selon Richard de Saint-Victor et Thomas d'Aquin," *Revue des sciences philosophiques et théologiques*, 92 (2008), 209-23. I confine myself solely to Aquinas's discussion of him in the tractate on the active and contemplative lives.

Christian tradition that had largely absorbed what it wanted of others, including the philosophical schools of Greece, and had already redirected it by way of infused virtues and gifts. Yet natural or philosophical contemplation remains a stratum of the concept in play, and this needs to be acknowledged.

In the early Latin West θεωρία is translated as *contemplatio*. The Latin word comes to us from Cicero: *Summa vero vis infinitatis et magna ac diligenti contemplatione dignissima est* ["The mighty power of the infinite is most worthy of great and loving contemplation"].[8] That Cicero introduces the word in *De natura deorum* suggests that it comes bearing religious significance, and that it enters Latin by way of Cicero perhaps guarantees sufficient awareness of its philosophical heritages.[9] Yet the new word also brings elements of popular Roman religious culture with it, specifically the determinations of *auspicia* as pronounced

8   See Cicero, *De natura deorum*, 1.50. Translation slighted adjusted. Also see Tacitus, *Annals*, 15.63.
9   One thinks, for instance, of *De finibus*, the *Tusculanæ disputationes*, *De fato*, *Paradoxa stoicorum*, and the (mostly) lost *Hortensius*.

by the augers, which could not have been far from Cicero's mind when he coined the word. He was a member of the College of Augers, after all, even though he was skeptical about the existence of the gods and therefore dubious about belief in divination. In *De divinatione* we find arguments against *auspicia*.[10] Auguries had been important for the Republic even so, and Cicero knew very well that its institutions needed to be preserved in a moderated way for the sake of good order.

There were two main kinds of auguries, those signaled spontaneously by the gods (*oblativa*) and those reckoned as given by the gods in answer to requests (*imperativa*). Auguries were given in many ways, though the earliest

10  See Cicero, *De diviniatione*, Part 2. Also see J. P. F. Wynne, *Cicero on the Philosophy of Religion: On the Nature of the Gods and On Divination* (Cambridge: Cambridge University Press, 2020). Wynne argues that Roman *religio* was less about right belief than about right practice, and that Cicero was in favor of moderating religion by philosophical inquiry, preserving it from superstition, on the one hand, and impiety, on the other. See *Cicero*, 72, 272.

practice must surely have been *ex avibus*, by way of the flight of birds, since the word *auspicium* comes from *avis* (bird) and *spicere* (to look at).[11] In order to look for propitious signs for a decision, with respect to a military campaign or the likelihood of abundant spring crops, recourse was made either to an established *templum* in the northern part of the Forum or to a new one that was drawn by members of the college, each with a *lituus* (much like a modern bishop's crozier but much shorter) that was used to stipulate the four corners of a square in the sky.[12] How a bird flew into the *templum* would give a trained auger the clues he needed. Not all birds could be counted as bearing signs,

11   There were five ways in which auspices were determined: *ex caelo, ex avibus, ex tripudiis, ex quadrupedibus,* and *ex diris.* See William Smith, ed., *A Dictionary of Greek and Roman Antiquities* (London: John Murray, 1875), 174-79.

12   See Cyril Bailey, *Phases in the Religion of Ancient Rome* (Oxford: Oxford University Press, 1932), 160-62. Varro tells us that *templum* derives from *tueri* "to gaze," *De lingua latina,* 7.7. Seneca remarks that the human body, with a head on top of a body, is made for contemplation. See his *De otio,* 5.4.

but the eagle was one that most certainly could, for it was known as Jupiter's bird. The Latin word *contemplatio*, along with our English word "contemplation," perpetually reminds us of the *templum* in the sky, the birds that flew through it, and what the activities in the sacred space might mean for the present and future.

Θεωρία and *contemplatio* bring somewhat different pagan heritages in tow, then, and inevitably both of them are changed when they entered the growing world of Christianity. The main object of contemplation changes; it is not the Forms or the intelligible structures of reality so much as the Trinity. Another important shift is the Christian emphasis on μετάνοια and thereafter steady moral purification of the one who seeks to contemplate the divine.[13]

---

13  Needless to say, the Romans engaged in purification before rituals. See, for instance, Cicero, *De legibus,* 2.19. Christians differed from Romans not in their regard for purity before sacrifice but in what "purity" meant to them and how to achieve it, namely, by a heartfelt moral reform of life, followed by study and devotion to prayer, all of which requires divine grace.

Origen (*c.* 185-254) tells us that the Canticle should be read last in a course of scriptural inquiry, "that a man may come to it when his manner of life has been purified" and only when he has become "competent to proceed to dogmatic and mystical matters" he may advance to the "contemplation [*contemplatio*] of the Godhead with pure and spiritual love."[14] Similarly, Gregory of Nyssa (*c.* 335-94?) speaks in his *Vita Moysis* of the need for the one who approaches "the contemplation [θεωρία] of Being" to be purified.[15] Contemplation is not open to everyone; it comes only after repentance and moral reform, study and a strict discipline of prayer that is maintained by faith and conducted in hope and love. Augustine will be in accord. (Incidentally, he

---

14   Origen, *The Song of Songs: Commentary and Homilies*, trans. and annotation R. P. Lawson (New York: The Newman Press, 1956), 44. The translation is of Rufinus's Latin translation of the mostly lost original Greek text.

15   See Gregory of Nyssa, *The Life of Moses*, trans. and intro. Abraham J. Malherbe and Everett Ferguson, pref. John Meyendorff (New York: Paulist Press, 1978), 92.

grants a limited role in Christianity to auguries, for he thinks that God speaks to us in many ways, including by lots, by stars, and through dreams.[16]) In *De trinitate* he tells us, "Contemplation in fact is the reward [*merces*] of faith, a reward for which hearts are cleansed through faith, as it is written, *cleansing their hearts through faith* (Acts 15: 9)."[17] The Latin tradition is consolidated and extended by Gregory the Great in his oceanic *Moralia in Job* where we learn that contemplation involves raising the eyes to light, that it is prompted by wonder, that the attuned mind

---

16 See Augustine, *Sermons*, 1, trans. Edmund Hill, ed. John E. Rotelle, The Works of Saint Augustine (New York: New City Press, 1990), 12.4. Yet also see *Confessions*, trans. and intro. Henry Chadwick (Oxford: Oxford University Press, 1991), 4.2.3. William E. Klingshirn discusses the issue in his "Divination and the Disciplines of Knowledge according to Augustine," *Augustine and the Disciplines: From Cassiciacum to Confessions*, ed. Karla Pollmann and Mark Vessey (Oxford: Oxford University Press, 2005), 113-40.

17 Augustine, *The Trinity*, trans., and intro. Edmund Hill, ed. John E. Rotelle (Brooklyn: New City Press, 1991), 1.17.

trembles when it is raised, and that even the most practiced monk is never perfect in his interior devotion.[18]

Augustine develops his theology of contemplation in an elliptical orbit of Platonism and Scripture and does so in the midst of seeking to establish the correspondence of the *imago dei* and the triune life of God. Yet Gregory looks elsewhere than the concord of Greek philosophy and Paul's letters, or,

18  See Gregory the Great, *MJ*, 1.25.34, 2.7.10, 5.32.56, and 5.36.66. Gregory's work had extensive influence in the middle ages, as is suggested by, among other things, Peter of Waltham's digest of it, *Remediarum conversorum*, which is extant in seventeen manuscripts. See Peter of Waltham, *Remediarium conversorum: A Synthesis in Latin of "Moralia in Job" by Gregory the Great*, ed. Joseph Gildea (Villanova: Villanova University Press, 1984). Gregory reflects further on contemplation in his other biblical commentaries. See his *On the Song of Songs*, trans. and intro. Mark DelCogliano (Collegeville, MI: Liturgical Press, 2012) and *Homilies on the Book of the Prophet Ezekiel*, trans. Theodosia Tomkinson, intro. Chrysostomos of Etna (Etna, CA: Center for Traditionalist Orthodox Studies, 2008).

rather, he assumes that it has been nicely achieved, and finds *contemplatio* by way of the allegorical hermeneutic when applied to the Hebrew Scriptures. The semantic fields of several Hebrew words overlap those of θεωρία and *contemplatio*, but none of these words has either the strong visual element or the appeal to raising the eyes that one finds in the Greek and Latin. There is *darash* ("to seek" or "to inquire"), *bikkesh* ("to seek"), *machashabah* ("thought"), and *siach* and *hagah* ("to muse" and "to meditate" respectively).[19] The closest, perhaps, is *hagah*, which alludes to wordless sounds, like a lion's growl or a human groan, and its association with meditation (in a non-Stoic sense) probably comes from the way in which someone brooding on a passage of Scripture will mumble its words over and over. We think of *lectio divina*, which is often a preparation for contemplation (and which can involve *contemplatio* itself). No one has seen this relation more clearly than John Scotus Eriugena (*c.* 815-*c.* 77) who contends

19   See Ecc. 1:13, 7: 25; Ps. 94:11; Ps. 104: 34, Ps. 119: 97, Ps. 1:2.

that Scripture was made for the human mind, not the other way round, for attentive reading of Scripture leads us back to our lost ability to contemplate God and presumably stimulates our desire to regain it.[20] With that said, it needs to be recalled that much Christian theology of both activities finds a ground in a typical or moral reading of the Hebrew Scriptures that a literal reading of those Scriptures would not support.[21] It also needs to be kept in mind that Gregory worked from the Vulgate, and sometimes the Vetus Latina, not from the original Hebrew.[22]

More generally, when Christians read or say "contemplation," we are convoking and changing Greek religious and philosophical practices, along with Roman religious practices, while also appropriating the Hebrew

---

20  See John Scotus Eriugena, *De caelesti Ierarchia*, *PL*, 122.2.1.146c. Eriugena uses the word *reduceretur* when writing about being led back to our original state of contemplative wonder.

21  One exception is Hagar who, after encountering an angel, testifies, "Thou art a God of seeing [*ra'ah*]" (Gen. 16:13, RSV).

22  See *MJ*, "Letter to Leander," 5.

Scriptures in ways that Judaism would reject. A word which suggests tranquility, "contemplation" contains a history that is not free of the treacheries of translation and, within that, of hermeneutical torsion, and as we will see the contemplative life, whether or not it is conducted within a religious order, is not always as peaceful as we might be led to believe; it is a struggle, as well as a graced achievement.[23] That last adjective indicates another major adjustment to the pagan understanding of θεωρία or *contemplatio*: it is not something that human beings can practice just by ourselves. One must be transformed by divine love in order to gaze upon that love.

*

One of the most impressive attempts to overcome the divisions in θεωρία or *contemplatio* is a treatise by Richard of St. Victor, *De arca mystica*, which is also known as *Benjamin*

---

23  See, for instance, Aquinas, *ST*, 2a2æ q.180 art. 7 ad 2.

*major* and *De gratia contemplationis*.[24] In formal terms, it is a tropological exegesis of Exod. 25: 8-40, the instructions the Lord gives to Moses how to build the Ark of the Covenant. Yet thematically it dilates on contemplation, both natural and infused. That Richard takes the ancient philosophers overly to restrict themselves to natural phenomena and to ignore the divine reality behind them is evident to any reader.[25] His interest in nature is in the first creation as a way of seeking our re-creation in Christ. If

24  The treatise, entitled *De gratia contemplationis, seu Benjamin Major* by J.-P. Migne in the *Patrologia Latina*, vol. 196, cols. 63-192, is edited as the *De contemplatione (Beniamin maior)*, but is also known as *De arca mystica (The Mystical Ark)* and the *De arca Moysi (The Ark of Moses)*. It is preceded in Migne, vol. 196, cols. 1-63 by *De præparatione animi ad contemplationem, liber dictus Benjamin minor*. Both works were translated into English from the Migne text by Grover A. Zinn, The Classics of Western Spirituality (New York: Paulist Press, 1979). His title and translation for the treatise on contemplation, *The Mystical Ark*, will be used here.

25  See, for instance, *MA*, 2.9.

we take "philosophy" more broadly, as φιλοσοφία, the endless task of understanding what is, how we know it, and how we should act, we can see that his vision of contemplation integrates what would otherwise be the philosophical and the religious by way of specific approaches to phenomena and the deity and the manners in which those approaches are made.

Like Hugh of St. Victor (*d.* 1141) before him, Richard distinguishes thinking, meditating, and contemplating.[26] "By means of inconstant and slow feet, thinking wanders here and there in all directions without any regard for arriving. Meditation presses forward with great activity of soul, often through arduous and rough places, to the end of the way it is going. Contemplation, in free flight, circles around with marvelous quickness wherever impulse moves it [*Contemplatio libero volatu quocunque eam fert impetus mira agilitate circumfertur*]." Richard is at once terse and lyrical:

26  Hugh introduces the distinction in the first of his homilies on Ecclesiastes, *PL*, 175, 116d-117d.

Thinking crawls; meditation marches and often runs; contemplation flies around everywhere and when it wishes suspends itself in the heights. [*Cogitatio serpit, meditatio incedit et ut multum currit. Contemplatio autem omnia circumvolat, et cum voluerit se in summis librat.*] Thinking is without labor and fruit; in meditation there is labor with fruit; contemplation continues without labor but with fruit. In thinking there is wandering; in meditation, investigation; in contemplation, wonder [*admiratio*]. Thinking is from imagination; meditation from reason; contemplation, from understanding.[27]

The motif of freedom with respect to contemplation is longstanding and irreducible: for Iamblichus (245-325), who

27   See *MA*, 4.5. Bonaventure will develop the taxonomy so that it consists of meditation, prayer and contemplation in his influential *De triplici via*.

early on asterisks the motif, the man given to θεωρία is "the most free," and although the Syrian philosopher is writing about Pythagoras he has Plato in mind, and plainly wishes to give his ideas as long and as rich a heritage as possible so as to bolster their authority.[28] For his part, Richard understands contemplation to be a Grace that God freely bestows, and that allows one freely to delve more deeply into being than thinking and meditating afford. It is "the free, more penetrating gaze of a mind, suspended with wonder concerning manifestations of wisdom."[29]

When Aquinas, a friar of the Order of Preachers and therefore committed to the

---

28  See Iamblichus, *On the Pythagorean Way of Life*, ed. John Dillon and Jackson Hershbell (Atlanta: Scholars Press, 1991), ch. 12. In the Latin West Boethius says something similar. See his *De consolatione philosophiæ*, 5.2. It should be pointed out that the motif was common in the ancient world. Seneca, for instance, writes of the intimacy of God and freedom in *De vita beata*, 15.7.

29  See Richard of St. Victor, *MJ*, 1.4. Clearly, Richard is adapting Hugh of St. Victor's definition of contemplation in his *In Ecclesiasten homiliæ*, 1, *PL*, 17, 117a.

mixed life, comes to weigh contemplation in *Summa theologiæ* 2a2æ q.180 art. 4 ad 3 he passes very quickly through the six distinctions that Richard draws; and this speed is itself worthy of note, as we shall see in a moment, once some clarifications have been made.[30] For Richard, contemplation turns on the imagination, reason, and understanding, where "imagination" names the ability to perceive something through its image so that, in turn, it can be rendered universal by reason. Contemplation, he says, falls into six kinds, each of which has divisions.[31] It can take place in the imagination and according to it (with respect to corporeal things), in the imagination as monitored by reason (with regard to

---

30  For Aquinas's affirmation of the mixed life over the contemplative and active lives, see *ST*, 2a2æ q.188 art. 6 *responsio*.

31  Richard of St. Victor, *MA*, 6. The Platonic origin of the division has been detailed by J.-A. Robillard in his "Les six genres de la contemplation chez Richard de Saint-Victor et leur origine platonicienne," *Revue des Sciences philosophiques et théologiques*, 28 (1939), 229-33. Richard's distinctions surely influenced Bonaventure in his *Itinerarium mentis in deum*.

the ordering of corporeal things), in reason according to the imagination (for reflecting on the passage from the visible to the invisible), in reason and regulated by reason (to do with invisible things that are beyond the reach of the imagination), above reason but not contrary to it (turning on what divine illumination tells us and that makes sense to us), and finally above reason and contrary to it (such as the doctrine of the Trinity).

The levels of contemplation are of prime importance, but it needs to be underlined that *De arca mystica* is a highly coded text in diverse registers. Richard cues the levels to the materials and figures of the ark: wood, gilding, crown, mercy seat, first cherub and second cherub. Only the first two levels are in the realm of the visible; thereafter, we pass to invisible created things, and, from there, to invisible and uncreated things. He also takes care to note how the first three of these levels are natural (with the fourth shared between human effort and Grace) and the final two entirely supernatural. Nor is this all. The levels are themselves organized under the aegis of the Psalmist's exclamation: "O that I had wings like a dove! I would fly away and be at rest" (Ps. 55:6, RSV). There are three groups of twos, each associated with a particular type of wing. The first two levels are appropriate only to earthly animals, the second two suit heavenly animals, and the third two allow one to fly so as to experience the hidden things of God. They are also divided as to four sets of vision, that of the flesh, reason, understanding, and ecstasy. All these codes, to do with symbols, objects, characters, wings, and eyes, are interrelated. In addition, Richard speaks of modes in which the mind responds to what is given to it. Richard's sense of these modes is unusual, as is Aquinas's lack of response to them, but this will concern us a little later.

Aquinas would have been familiar with such elaborate symbolic coding, which had been sanctioned by Pseudo-Dionysius the Areopagite's remarks in *De coelesti hierarchia* on the symbol's power to uplift the spirit and the importance of symbols even when they are unlike what they symbolize.[32] Such

32 See Pseudo-Dionysius the Areopagite, *De coelesti hierarchia*, 1 and 2.

symbolism had become common in mystical treatises of the twelfth and thirteenth centuries, and it would not of itself have detained Aquinas when working out his own theology of contemplation. Yet it should serve to slow us down when reading both authors. When Aquinas considers Richard's divisions, as he does in 2a2æ q.180 art. 4, he swivels away from him by way of the *sed contra*, and this is the first place where we need to stop briefly and weigh what is happening. The pivot is Gregory the Great's statement in the *Moralia in Job* that "In contemplation indeed it is the beginning or God that is sought [*quod in contemplatione principium, quod Deus est, quaeritur*]."[33] The sentence allows Aquinas to divide what is primary from what is secondary in contemplation.[34]

---

33  Gregory is presumably alluding to John 8: 25 as rendered in the Vulgate: *dicebant ergo ei tu quis es dixit eis Iesus principium quia et loquor vobis.*

34  Gregory the Great, *MJ*, 2.6.37, 61. Also see Aquinas, *Commentary on the Gospel of St. Matthew*, trans. Paul M. Kimball (NP: Dolorosa Press, 2012), 5:10. Aquinas could well have cited Augustine, *De doctrina Christiana*, 1.2 in support of his view.

Richard is not misguided, Aquinas thinks, when he finds suitable objects of contemplation in nature and the intellect, but these identify stages of an ascent which, when achieved, perfects the intellect. Nor does Aquinas disregard the beauty of the created order, although he favors the active use of the mind over its passive reception of form in appreciating beauty, for it is that which directs one to God. The secondary nature of much that attracts Richard in *De arca mystica* accounts for the celerity with which Aquinas passes through the six stages.

We may well question Aquinas's reliance on Gregory's authoritative statement in the all-important fulcrum of the *sed contra*, for Gregory also tells us in the *Moralia in Job* that contemplation does not have an object that sheers away everything on the way to it. "The aim of contemplation," he writes, "should be such that it passes from the consideration [*consideranda*] of a few to the many and from the many to all things, inasmuch as it is led to move gradually, and by embracing all that is transitory it determines them and, itself nearly incomprehensible, goes on growing."[35] So Aquinas differs from Gregory in a signal manner. When reflecting on whether there are discrete activities in the contemplative life, he tells us that while that life has only one activity, gazing upon the truth, it is subtended by others. "Some of these have to do with the understanding of principles from which one proceeds to contemplation of truth; others with the deduction from those principles to the truth one seeks to know" (2a2æ q.180 art. 3 *responsio*). Where Gregory stresses that the aim of contemplation is inclusive, Aquinas places the accent on gradual exclusion until just one pure gaze is left, and where Gregory reflects on natural phenomena Aquinas has in mind the grasping of intellectual principles. Later in the same commentary, Gregory observes that David contemplated his mortal condition and Paul his weakness; and for Aquinas these acts would not be contemplation as such but rather exercises of the

35  Gregory the Great, *MJ*, 17.9.11.

moral virtues, which will dispose one to gaze upon the deity.[36]

These two counterexamples from Gregory suggest that, in part at least, he harmonizes as readily with Richard as with Aquinas, and we realize the troubles of selecting just one line about *contemplatio* from a text that attends to it now and then over some 1800 pages of commentary on Job. Had Aquinas chosen the passage about the need to contemplate the many from the *Moralia* for the *sed contra* to 2a2æ q.180 art. 4 we might have acquired a more generous account of Richard's vision of contemplation, one that does not consign attention to the natural world to secondary concerns; but Aquinas's discussion of contemplation is informed by the sheer momentum of the *Summa theologiæ*, which includes the energy harnessed by the discussions of the beatific vision (1a q.12), the gifts of the Holy Spirit (1a2æ q.68 and again in 2a2æ with respect to theological and cardinal virtues), Grace, both habitual and

36 Gregory the Great, *MJ*, 23.27.53; Aquinas, *ST*, 2a2æ q.180 art. 2 *responsio*.

*auxilium* (1a2æ qq.106-14), the infused virtues (2a2æ qq.1-46) and of course rapture (2a2æ q.175). It would be naïve not to expect at least one principle of selection operating as he works, one that is more finely determined and more concrete as the treatise goes along, even if it is never explicitly stated.[37] At the same time, the portions I have retrieved from the *Moralia* at least serve to give us reason to keep in play Richard on contemplation as well as Aquinas. Not that Aquinas uses the *sed contra* as a knock down argument, in the manner of Humpty Dumpty or analytic philosophers, but as a means of allowing an opposing view to enter his deliberations.[38] With the appearing of another

37  One possible principle might well be the thirty-fifth proposition of Proclus in his *Elements of Theology*: "Every thing caused, abides in, proceeds from, and returns, or is converted to, its cause," *Elements of Theology*, Prop. 35, in his *The Six Books of Proclus*, trans. Thomas Taylor (London: Law and Co., 1816).

38  Lewis Carroll, *Through the Looking-Glass: And what Alice Saw There* (Chicago: Homewood Pub., 1902), 95.

possible view, motivated by authority or reason, we have the pedagogic opportunity for theology to become a site of critical thinking, not magisterial judgment. The *responsio* will allow for what is introduced by the *sed contra* to become more fully apparent within its limits, usually by way of one or more distinctions, by which I mean more than *distinctio* (the medieval Latin word for a section of a text), namely, ways of mental division so as to receive and organize phenomena in specific situations and to particular ends.

Even a passing reflection on distinctions is enough to warrant a pause to ponder the varied types that have already been introduced, and to notice the individual theological styles of Richard and Aquinas in how they are made. Recognitions of difference do not form themselves; they require the pressure of circumstances to be delineated, that pressure being a felt need to pass from obscurity to clarity, sometimes by way of overcoming an ambiguity.[39] The divisions that we

39  I am indebted to Robert Sokolowski's essay "Making Distinctions" in his *Pictures, Quota-*

come to trust and that remain with us are those in which the arrangement of terms manifests phenomena. We say to ourselves that the syntax of being is respected by the person separating terms, or we say that a differentiation is merely linguistic or mental and has no roots in experience; and in this way we discriminate between drawing and constructing a distinction.[40] So, when Hugh and Richard tell us that we should separate thinking, meditating and contemplating, we are inclined to agree with them, and perhaps even to admit the perspicacity with which Richard, in particular, does so.[41] We might

tions, and Distinctions: Fourteen Essays in Phenomenology (Notre Dame: University of Notre Dame Press, 1992), 55-92, as well as to Richard Robinson's Definition (Oxford: Clarendon Press, 1950).

40  This difference is sometimes known as the two distinctions of reason, one with grounds in reality and the mind and the other with a ground just in the mind.

41  See Richard, MA, 1.4. I should also mention Achard of St. Victor who is also finely attuned to making distinctions. See, for instance, his De unitate et pluralitate creaturarum, 4. The text is sometimes also known as De trinitate.

also acknowledge that wobbly lines can rightly be drawn between imagining, reasoning and understanding, especially once we grasp what these words signified in the twelfth century; but when Richard continues and tells us that these three words generate six kinds of contemplation, each of which has sub-divisions, and that they have sundry neat groupings, let alone that they have disparate modes, we may well suspect that divisions are being constructed, and that phenomena are not being saved so much as being imagined. We will remember that Augustine was delighted by six being the lowest perfect number, since creation is grasped by human beings in six phases, and one might smile a little at the good fortune that accompanies the number six through the middle ages, which is rivaled only by that of the holy number seven.[42]

42  See Augustine, *The Literal Meaning of Genesis*, trans. Edmund Hill, in *On Genesis*, The Works of Saint Augustine 1/13 (Hyde Park, NY: New City Press, 2002), 4.2-6. In the *Itinerarium mentis in deum* Bonaventure also favors the number six, on the ground that the seraph that Francis

If we are tempted to think in this way, we would do well to reflect that for Richard, as for other Christian thinkers of the early and medieval church, Scripture indicates how being is articulated. Divine illumination, when properly interpreted, tells us things about reality that unaided reason cannot.[43] This doubling of

saw in a vision had six wings. The seraphim in Is. 6: 2 have four faces and six wings, as does the seraph in 2 Enoch 21: 1. As an index of the favor given to the number six, I list some of the figures common in the twelfth and thirteenth centuries: six days of creation, six works of mercy, six ministering spirits, and six modes of brotherly love. Similarly, for the number seven: seven gifts of the Holy Spirit, seven spiritual deserts, seven modes of confession, seven joys, and three lots of seven with respect to contemplation (seven purgative contemplations, seven illuminative contemplations and seven perfective contemplations). Biblical numbers are not simply mathematical numbers; they are symbols and to be interpreted as such.

43 The very model of the ark of the covenant, along with the two cherubim, is a prime example; but also see Richard's divisions between Moses, Bezeleel and Aaron when introducing the three modes of contemplation in *MA*, 5.1.

nature and the sacred (whether by way of salvation history or biblical symbolism) con-
tributes to the range and character of
manifestation, as Richard understands it, and,
indeed, how others who came after him fig-
ured it as well. Bonaventure in the *Breviloquium*, for instance, details the plurality of
manifestations of God in and through Scripture, which he details in terms of its breadth,
length, height, depth and modes.[44] Richard's
way of disclosing phenomena is, as we shall
see in a moment, rather different from
Aquinas's. But before I take a step in the direction of clarifying Richard, there is a preliminary
matter to address, which could muddy the
path ahead unless it is settled now. Is Richard
indeed speaking of contemplation at all, at
least in the sense that Aquinas has in mind?

Aquinas thinks that contemplation is

---

44  See Bonaventure, *Breviloquium*, intro., trans. and
    notes Dominic V. Monti, Works of St. Bonaventure
    (St. Bonaventure, NY: Franciscan Institute, 2005),
    1.5. The account of the dimensions of Scripture is
    given in the prologue. On the theme of manifes-
    tation, see Emmanuel Falque, *Saint Bonaventure et
    l'entrée de Dieu en Théologie* (Paris: Vrin, 2001).

limited to God as the proper object of our love, a claim that is also a mild criticism of Richard.[45] For it seems right that only God, who is inexhaustible, can sustain our contemplation. Dante offers the same criticism when, in the tenth canto of the *Paradiso*, Richard is not regarded as a contemplative but as an advocate and practitioner of *consideratione*. Dante's Aquinas introduces Richard directly after Isidore and Bede as follows: *e di Riccardo, / che a considerar fu più che viro* ("and Richard / who in consideration was more than man").[46] The blessed souls that Dante recognizes as *contemplativi*

45 It is not the only time: Aquinas prizes Pseudo-Dionysius's economic understanding of the movements of contemplation over Richard's apparently more capacious sense of the same activity. See *ST*, 2a2æ q. 180 art. 7 ad 3.

46 Dante, *Paradiso*, 10.131-32. Bonaventure, however, says that Richard "excels. . . in contemplating," *De reduction artium ad theologiam*, intro., commentary and trans. Emma Thérèse Healy (St. Bonaventure, NY: Franciscan Institute, 1955), 5. It should be noted that Dante is most likely alluding to *MA*, 4.1 and to Richard's expression there: *plus quam humanum*.

are encountered later, in the twenty-first and twenty-second cantos of the *Paradiso* and, as it happens, two of the most important of these souls, Peter Damian and Benedict, were active and contemplative at different stages of their lives. Peter (*d.* 1072) started religious life in the monastery of Fonte Avellana, which was first and foremost devoted to prayer (*che suol esser disposto a sola latria*) but in 1057 he was required by Stephen IX to serve as a cardinal. Benedict (480-543) founded twelve monastic communities, composed the *Regula Sancti Benedicti*, a founding document of the contemplative life, and established the great monastery of Monte Cassino.[47] Their examples will give local habitations and names to Aquinas's convictions, especially about ecclesial states of life (as opposed to modes of life), which seems to be a distinction original to him, but long before returning to them I would like

47  See Dante, *Paradiso*, 21.82-142 for Peter Damian and, for Benedict, *Paradiso*, 22.28-99. Benedict is accompanied by Maccarius and Romoaldus, who were wholly given to contemplation.

to circle back to the word that Dante's Aquinas uses to identify Richard's practice.

*Consideratione* perhaps originates in Roman augury (maybe deriving from *sidus, sider-*: star, constellation), and it already occurs in Gregory's *Moralia in Job*, as we have seen.[48] Any lingering pagan connotations of the word were overridden by the influence of Bernard of Clairvaux's *De consideratione* (completed *c.* 1153) where we find an emphasis on using the senses and sensible things in an ordered and social way to serve God.[49] Yet here Bernard is drawn neither to the created world nor to ascent, and Richard is intent on both.[50] The word *consideratio* and its forms are used frequently by Richard,

48  One also finds the word in Augustine — in *De trinitate*, 10.10.14, for example — but without the sharpness of definition that Bernard gives to it.

49  Bernard of Clairvaux, *Five Books on Consideration: Advice to a Pope*, trans. John Anderson and Elizabeth T. Kennan (Kalamazoo, MI: Cistercian Publication, 1976), 1.7.8, 2.2.5-7.

50  For Bernard on ascent, specifically on contemplation as ecstasy, see his *Sermons on the Song of Songs*, 3: *Sermons 47-66* (Kalamazoo, MI: Cistercian Publications, 1979), 53.

and if we examine the practice as he commends it to us we will see that it prepares us for *contemplatio* and even overlaps with it a little.[51] So, Dante's Aquinas is not exactly unfair to Richard, even if he seems a tad ungenerous to him.[52] For his part, in accenting contemplation

51  See Bernard of Clairvaux, *Five Books on Consideration*, 2.2.5. It needs to be remembered that, as Bernard of Clairvaux stresses, there should be *consideratio* of the self as well as of situations. See *Five Books on Consideration*, 2.3.6. Consideration continues in the tradition to be associated with contemplation. See, for instance, the seventeenth-century divine, Richard Baxter, *The Saints' Everlasting Rest* (New York: American Tract Society, 1824), ch. 14. On the overlap of the words "meditation" and "contemplation" in the seventeenth century, see Louis L. Martz, *The Poetry of Meditation: A Study of English Religious Literature of the Seventeenth Century* (New Haven: Yale University Press, 1954), 16-20.

52  One needs to recall, however, that Richard does not draw hard and fast distinctions between consideration and contemplation in *De arca mystica*, and also that, perhaps out of modesty, he demurs from speaking from experience about the higher reaches of contemplation. See *MA*, 1.10 and 5.19. Bernard admits an overlap of *consideratio* and *contemplatio*. See *Five Books on*

as ascent, Aquinas follows only three of Richard's four metaphors for the act. There are wings of contemplation, a watchtower of understanding, and a ladder of contemplation: all metaphors of verticality.[53] The fourth metaphor is the mirror, which Richard takes to be the rational soul. "For if the invisible things of God are seen, being understood by the intellect by means of those things which have been made (cf. Rom. 1: 20), where, I ask, have the traces of knowledge been found more clearly imprinted than in His image?"[54] The Pauline mirror of contemplation (1 Cor. 13:12) is a metaphor of horizontal vision, whether it be a *speculum* or a *specularia*, and it is significant, for it applies to the first three levels of contemplation.[55]

*Consideration*, 2.2.5. Even though he alludes to Bernard on just this point, Aquinas aligns *consideratio* with *meditatio*. See *ST*, 2a2æ q. 180 art. 3 ad 1.

53  See Richard of St. Victor, *MA*, 1.10; *MA*, 5. 4; *De trinitate*, prologue.

54  Richard of St. Victor, *Benjamin minor*, 72.

55  See Richard of St. Victor, *MA*, 1.6. Also see *Benjamin minor*, 72. On the *specularia* or window made of mica, see Pliny the Elder, *Naturalis historiæ*, 36.64-67 and Seneca, *Epistulæ*, 90.

There can be no question that Richard prizes ascent: his tropological exegesis of Exod. 25: 8-40 passes from one symbol to a higher one, from wood to gilding to crown to the mercy seat, and from there to the first cherub and finally to the second cherub. The two cherubs gaze at one another and in that apparently empty space between them God abides and, more, has promised to speak to Moses from there (Exod. 25: 22). Nonetheless, we might reflect that one in four of Richard's metaphors is horizontal. When Aquinas considers this metaphor, he quickly assigns it to meditation, not contemplation.[56] Even so, we might speculate whether Richard's allegory of the ark of the covenant can be read horizontally as well as vertically, and, if so, if it allows us to rest in the ascent in order to contemplate the good things that God has created in the natural world and for the exercise of the intellect.[57] To adopt a vocabulary

56  See Aquinas, *ST*, 2a2æ q. 180 art. 3 ad 2.
57  See Richard of St. Victor, "Commentary on Psalm 113," *Collected Works of Richard of St. Victor* (Brandon, FL: Revelation Insight Pub. Co., 2016), no pagination.

that is not Richard's own, and that introduces complexities of its own, does contemplation include the Kingdom as well as the King?

\*

This question immediately prompts another: What is the Kingdom? Or, better, how does the Kingdom appear? It is not always manifest in the same way, and in some medieval theology it barely appears at all, at least not by name. One reason is because, in the twelfth century, explicit theologies of the Kingdom risked being edged into bitter theo-political controversy. A clear index is the reception of Joachim of Fiore's theology of history, presented in his *Expositio in Apocalypsim* (completed *c.* 1196-99).[58] History, he thinks, has a trinitarian shape: the Age of the Father, which corresponds to the Old Testament; the Age of

---

58  See Joachim of Fiore, *Expositio in Apocalypsim* (rpt. Frankfurt am Main: Minerva, 1964). Also see his *Enchiridion super Apocalypsim*, ed. and intro. Edward Kilan Burger (Toronto: Pontifical Institute of Mediæval Studies, 1986). Joachim's theology of history turned on his reading of Rev. 14:6.

the Son, which stems from the first and begins with the New Testament and will run until a decisive, upsetting event of 1260; and the Age of the Holy Spirit, which is generated by both ages, in which the spirit will triumph over the letter in all respects, and which will be a Kingdom of contemplation.[59] The Fourth Lateran Council (1215) condemned Joachim's teachings, and Aquinas responds critically to his understanding of the Trinity in 1a q. 38 art. 5.[60] Dante, however, regards him as a prophet and places him in paradise.[61]

---

59  See Marjorie Reeves, *Joachim of Fiore and the Prophetic Future* (London: SPCK, 1976) and Bernard McGinn, *The Calabrian Abbot: Joachim of Fiore in the History of Western Thought* (New York: Macmillan, 1985). It is important to stress that Joachim did not propose to abandon either Testament; rather, the third age or *status* would come about through a spiritual understanding of Scripture. Equally important to stress is that Joachim's theology of history is not straightforwardly linear.

60  See *Denz.*, 431-33.

61  See Dante, *Paradiso*, 12: 140-41. For Aquinas's distaste for Joachim's works, see McGinn, *The Calabrian Abbot*, 209-13.

If the Kingdom does not always appear by name in the twelfth and thirteenth centuries, it tends to become manifest under other descriptions and in various ways. There is, of course, the original Kingdom of Creation in which Adam and Eve are, in effect, deemed to be of royal lineage. This Kingdom is no sooner established than it is lost; and although there come to be Judges and Kings in Israel, while there are enthronement psalms of considerable power (Ps. 24, 47, 93, 95-100), and while the theme of the Kingdom resonates throughout Isaiah, it is only definitively revived by Christ's preaching of the Kingdom of God. Finally, those who accept what Jesus preaches may hope to encounter the Kingdom in its eschatological dimension, the state of intimacy with the Trinity that we call "heaven." These three senses make it difficult to know exactly what "Kingdom" means when it is used without qualification; and matters are made much worse because when Jesus speaks of it he seems to denote a multi-stable phenomenon. The Kingdom is within as well as without; it is here now and yet is still to come; and it is weak while also strong.[62]

Aquinas does not engage the theme of the Kingdom in a systematic manner. One looks in vain through the great *Summæ* for discussions of it.[63] But it appears brightly in his commentary on Matthew, which speaks repeatedly of the Kingdom, and in his commentaries on the letters of Paul. Unsurprisingly, perhaps, Aquinas mostly approaches the Kingdom eschatologically: it appears most surely in and through the promise of God finally being all in all and, more particularly, in the Last Judgment when an irrevocable decision is made between the carnal

---

62 The situation almost guarantees a complex reception history of the Kingdom. See Ernst Staehelin, *Die Verkündigung des Reiches Gottes in der Kirche Jesu Christi: Zeugnisse aus allen Jahrhunderten und allen Konfessionen*, 7 vols (Basel: F. Reinhardt, 1951-65).

63 The *Index Thomisticus* supplies references of all occurrences of *regnum dei* and *regnum caelorum*, including those in the *Summa theologiæ*. The expressions occur quite often; discussion of the theme is far more restricted in the corpus and is found mainly in the Scriptural commentaries.

and the spiritual.[64] The Kingdom, as he says, consists in contemplation in eternity.[65] The Kingdom is not a theme for Richard; however, it is quietly present throughout *Benjamin minor*, which is also known as *De præparatione animi ad contemplationem*, chiefly in the elaboration of the meaning of Leah as virtue. In *De arca mystica* it appears more eschatologically, in that the contemplative must forge angelic wisdom and thereby be one with the angelic hierarchy in order to hear God speak to him or her. Also, though, it appears more subtly in the commendation to contemplate God in the created order in all its levels, regardless of the stage of ascent.

---

64  See Aquinas, *Commentary on the Gospel of St. Matthew,* 5:19, 7: 21. Aquinas is well aware of other ways of understanding the Kingdom. See, for instance, his remarks on Matt. 11:11 and his reading of "Kingdom" as believers in Christ in *Commentary on the Letters of Saint Paul to the Corinthians,* trans. F. R. Larcher, B. Mortensen and D. Keating, ed. J. Mortensen and E. Alarcón (Lander, WY: Aquinas Institute for the Study of Sacred Doctrine, 2012), 1 Cor. 15: 24.

65  Aquinas, *Commentary on the Gospel of St. Matthew,* 8: 11-12.

\*

We may regard Richard's treatise as an invitation to consider the sheer reach of contemplation in daily life, how each and every aspect of the created world, our intellectual engagement with it, as well as the Creator in his acts and even his essence, offers itself to be tasted and enjoyed (Ps. 34:8). If we look at Richard's contemporaries, we can see how generous his account is. Bernard of Clairvaux, for one, accepts just four sorts of contemplation, each of which is rooted in Scripture, and each of which refers to God: the admiration of divine majesty (*admiratio majestatis*), the observation of divine judgment (*intuens judicia Dei*), the remembrance of blessings (*memoriam beneficiorum*), and the expectation of the fulfillment of divine promises, the meditation of eternity (*meditatio æternitatis*).[66] (Again, it will be noticed that the line between contemplation and meditation is a wavy and broken one.) In one sense,

---

66  See Bernard of Clairvaux, *Five Books on Consideration*, 5.14.32.

Richard posits a clear hierarchy of thinking, mediating and contemplating; yet, in another, wider sense, there is nothing excluded from contemplation. No change of object is required, only a shift of attitude. One passes from regarding and examining to marveling, all of which presumes the disciplined monastic life that is taught in the Abbey.[67]

Two things are worth noting at the outset. First, Richard says very little about repentance and purification of the heart before engaging in contemplation, no more than he does about the leisure needed for such a life. That is largely because he has already done so in *Benjamin minor*. There can be no question that, for Richard, one must prepare to contemplate anything by exercising the virtues. Second, and more intriguing, Richard excludes nothing in principle from contemplation; and this might give us pause, at least if we have been influenced by the tradition that comes to us from Shaftesbury, Kant and Schopenhauer.

---

67  See Richard of St. Victor, *MA*, 1.3. The verb Richard uses which is translated by "marvel" is *miramur*.

For we might object that some things resist being contemplated. Certainly, anything false appears ill suited to contemplation, although it may well fascinate us. Contemplation is cathected to the truth, which must be at least partly known, either naturally or by revelation.[68] Also, anything that immediately appeals to our appetites, such as food, drink and sex, does not seem to be open to contemplation of any kind or to any degree until the appetite for it has been curtailed or satisfied.[69] I might anticipate any one of these things, and revolve it in my mind, but whatever is anticipated is given as absent whereas whatever is contemplated is taken to be present, in one or another manner of presence.

To which one of Richard's defenders would respond: Presumably, all these desires have already been subject to the discipline of

68  See Bernard of Clairvaux, *Five Books on Consideration*, 2.2.5.

69  See Arthur Schopenhauer, *The World as Will and Representation*, 2 vols, ed. Christopher Janaway, trans. Judith Norman and Alistair Welchman (Cambridge: Cambridge University Press, 2014), 1, § 40.

the exercise of the virtues, and so they do not even occur to Richard in *De arca mystica*. Continuing the line of thought suggested by the objection, one might also reject the idea of contemplating anything repugnant — a rotting carcass, for instance — or even something that overpowers us, such as an encounter with the sublime.[70] As we gather such examples, we will be pressed to distinguish aesthetic contemplation from its religious counterpart. What is intolerable for the former is possible for the latter because of moral discipline and Grace. It might well be for our good to contemplate a rotting carcass, for example, and we know that the religious sublime can indeed amaze, astonish or confound the spiritually unprepared and even those who are well advanced along the way to God. One must be freed from sin in order to enjoy being suspended before God. So, another division in contemplation comes to our attention, the aesthetic and the religious, and it too will prove troublesome to overcome completely.

---

70  See Schopenhauer, *The World as Will and Representation*, 1, §§ 39-40.

For when it comes to contemplation, the aesthetic and the religious are not always so easy to separate as my example suggests; and this situation has long generated anxieties and even violence among some Christians who wish to keep the two strictly apart. Where Catholics and Orthodox have held that beauty or sublimity, in liturgy, poetry, the visual arts and music, can help to orient the soul to God, some of the Reformers have believed it to be a distraction in worship. One might contemplate the beauty of plainsong or an icon rather than the sovereign deity to whom they supposedly gesture. One might have a sublime experience of the *Dies ira* in Gregorian chant and be diverted from pondering one's sins and the judgment that awaits one. Indeed, it might be that art constitutively deflects our attention from moral and religious duties, in much the same way that Plato in book ten of the *Republic* feared that epic poetry might compromise the work of philosophy. In the nineteenth century French Symbolists argued that music and poetry direct us to ineffable heights in ways that prose and concepts simply cannot attain.[71] Yet a counterargument maintains that art points in the exact opposite direction; it involves us in magic and rhythm, pre-phenomenal, which neutralize our rapport with reality and inclines us to defer our moral and religious responsibilities. [72] If Schopenhauer is right to think that aesthetic contemplation allows for self-transcendence, even if only in peak experiences, and even if only momentarily, and that it gives us a degree of spiritual satisfaction in what we see, then aesthetic contemplation is competing on the same ground as its religious counterpart.[73]

---

71  On the ineffable, see in particular Vladimir Jankélévitch, *Music and the Ineffable*, trans. Carolyn Abbate (Princeton: Princeton University Press, 2013).

72  See, in particular, Emmanuel Levinas's essay "Reality and its Shadow," *Collected Philosophical Papers*, trans. Alphonso Lingis (The Hague: Martinus Nijhoff, 1987), 1-13. Also see the discussion of the issue in my *Poetry and Revelation: For a Phenomenology of Religious Poetry* (London: Bloomsbury, 2017), ch. 6.

73  See Jerrold Levinson, "Schopenhauer's Aesthetics," in his *Contemplating Art* (Oxford: Clarendon Press, 2006), esp. 361.

These concerns ripened only in the nineteenth and twentieth centuries, after the divorce of aesthetics and metaphysics. They did not upset Aquinas, for whom beauty means that which is pleasant to apprehend, and which does not generate a discipline other than metaphysics.[74] Nor did they bother Richard, in large part because for him even sensible objects reward us lavishly in their beauty when we turn our attention, informed by the Christian faith, on them. No doubt he thinks that created things, even very beautiful ones, are significantly dissimilar to the Creator. All the same, we may enjoy their way of being in order to approach the longed-for lands of likeness. A certain

---

74 See Aquinas, *ST*, 1a q.39 art. 8 *responsio* and 1a2æ, q. 27 art. 1 ad 3. The "pleasantness" in question consists of actuality, proportion, radiance, and integrity, and is associated with the Son. Also see Umberto Eco, *The Aesthetics of Thomas Aquinas*, trans. Hugh Bredin (Cambridge, MA: Harvard University Press, 1988). I leave aside here the complex question of whether beauty, for Aquinas, is a transcendental.

tranquility in the soul allows him to linger with created being and not speed past it. Of course, my expression "lands of likeness" alludes to Augustine's evocation of finding himself far from God in the *regio dissimiltudinis*, "the land of unlikeness"; but it is contemplation that leads the soul in its final stage from that region of alienation to the lands of likeness where the soul increasingly recognizes that like leads to like, that the *imago dei* leads to God.[75] The first of these lands would be within, where God's image shines, albeit dimly, and then one would progress on one's spiritual journey and would increasingly discern the power and the kindness of the divine reign.[76] Let us see how Richard

---

75   See Augustine, *Confessions*, 7.10.16. Augustine alludes to Plato, *Statesman*, 273d.

76   One finds a similar approach in Achard of St. Victor. See Achard of St. Victor, *Works*, trans. and intro. Hugh Feiss (Kalamazoo, MI: Cistercian Pub., 2001), 67, 248. Achard points out that above the land of likeness is the land of righteousness, and higher than this region is the land of beatitude, which is surmounted by the land of identity, which is the Holy Trinity. In general,

undertakes that journey. In following him from a distance, as it were, we can also test whether his distinctions rest on phenomenological evidence or are merely constructions consequent on the theology he learned at the Abbey of St. Victor.

When we gaze at a leaf, for example, we may take pleasure in its greenness, the patterning of its veins, its glossiness, its shape; we may feel the leaf's fine texture or regret the places where it is malformed, withered, or diseased. We may appreciate the abundance of leaves in Spring, Summer and Fall. Throughout, we are making images of the leaf, and considering only these. In doing so, however, we may almost unnoticeably pass to the second level of contemplation, the order in which sensible objects may be found. We may mull over the arrangement of the leaves in the tree, the organization of branches and the trunk, the shedding of seeds, and so on. Order, as

both Achard and Richard are indebted to Hugh of St. Victor. See his *In Ecclesiastem homiliæ*, 1, *PL*, 175, 117b.

Augustine had stressed, is the beginning of ascent.[77] Not that "ascent" here need mean for us just what it plainly meant for Augustine or anyone in his wake for whom one or another Platonic school provided intellectual guidance. We may not think of our curriculum leading us by magisterial pre-design to intellectual heights, and we may figure a vision of the One quite differently from the movement of the soul from *extra se* to *intra se* (as it was for Plotinus) and, from there, to *supra se* (as it was for

---

77  See Augustine, *On Order*, trans. and intro. Silvano Borruso (South Bend: St. Augustine's Press, 2007), 1.9.27. Augustine speaks in more detail of ascent in several places, most notably in *The Magnitude of the Soul*, trans. John J. McMahon, in *The Immortality of the Soul, Magnitude of the Soul, On Music, Advantage of Believing, Faith in Things Unseen* (Washington, DC: Fathers of the Church, 1947), 33. 70-76, *Confessions*, 7 and 9, *On Music*, 6, *True Religion*, trans. Edmund Hill, in *On Christian Belief*, ed. Boniface Ramsey, Works of Saint Augustine (New York: New City Press, 2005), 50. 98-99, and *Teaching Christianity*, trans. and notes Edmund Hill, ed. John E. Rotelle, Works of Saint Augustine (New York: New City Press, 1996), 2. 9-11.

Augustine).[78] "Ascent" can bespeak a reorientation of viewpoint such as happens when we moderns proceed from regarding the world as nature to reflecting on it as creation, that is, from the world as given to us through the lens of natural science to the world as given to us in terms of divine power. In this way, we can pass from lower to higher categorial kinds until we are summoned to that which has no kind at all. This rethinking of "ascent," which has a medieval precedent in William of Ockham's *Summa logicæ*, becomes clearer when we continue to think Richard's exegesis in terms that we moderns, including believers, find more familiar than those common in the monastic world of the twelfth century.[79]

---

78 See Plotinus, *Enneads*, 1.6.9.24-25 and Augustine *On Order*, 2, *On Music*, 6, and *Confessions*, 3.6.11.

79 See William of Ockham, *Summa logicæ*, ed. Philotheus Boehner, Gedeon Gál and Stephanus Brown, Opera Philosophia, 1 (St. Bonaventure, NY: Franciscan Institute, 1974), Cap. 70, *De divisionibus suppositionis personalis*.

To rise to the next level, reason according to the imagination, would be to reach from the visible to the invisible, to grasp the εἶδος of the tree, including its pattern of parts and whole. In going further, one would leave the guidance of sensuous images, and seize truths that have no physical image at all. For Richard, committed to an Augustinian epistemology, this requires Grace as well as human effort. Aquinas rethought this theory of knowledge so as to grant natural reason a space of its own. And for us who come after him (indeed, after the seventeenth century), this second stage of Richard's would involve reflecting on the chemical and physical structure of the tree. Today, it would call for study of the tree's morphology, which would require mathematical models to describe symmetry around the central axis, the calculus of variations for leaf density, as well as appeals to the Fibonacci sequence to understand the distribution of seeds and the arrangement of

80  See F. R. Yeatts, "Tree Shape and Branch Structure: Mathematical Models," *Mathematical and*

leaves.[80] This is the limit that natural science reaches and were we to pass to the fifth object of contemplation we would begin to gaze upon the tree as combining created elements as arranged in the periodical table. We would rise from what Augustine calls "evening knowledge," which was given to the angels first of all, the knowledge of the mathematical, physical and chemical structures of what had been created, to "morning knowledge," which was granted to them only afterwards, and which allowed them to taste God's deep love for all that he had created.[81] For Thomists, morning knowledge is above reason but not always contrary to it: for we can use the natural light of reason to

*Computational Forestry and Natural-Resource Sciences*, 4: 1 (2012), 2-15. Reading a scientific text such as this should make us smile less at Augustine's delight at the number six. Modern mathematical analysis is a long way from number mysticism, but at least Augustine, not to mention other Fathers, was right to think that numbers tell us a lot about creation.

81  See Augustine, *The Literal Meaning of Genesis,* Book 4.

establish that there is a creator God and even to conceive something of his love.[82] What one cannot do, though, is comprehend the triune nature of this God, the ground and abyss of his love, and understand what it means for the Father to love the world into being in and through Trinitarian action. To hover before triune love would be to have attained the highest level of contemplation, a status we cannot expect to sustain for long in this life but may hope to enjoy more fully in eternity.

So, according to Richard, everything in reality, whether created or uncreated, offers itself to human contemplation as well as to meditation and thought. There is nothing so small or so banal that it does not respond to a free attentive gaze that has been educated in the faith and that begins directing

---

82  For Aquinas on these two modes of knowledge, see *ST*, 1a q. 58 art. 6, 7.

83  See Richard of St. Victor, *The Book of Notes*, 2.2, in *Interpretation of Scripture: Theory*, ed. Franklin T. Harkins and Frans van Liere, Victorine Texts in Translation (Turnhout, Belgium: Brepols, 2012), 310.

us to spiritual levels of being.[83] Even a single leaf can, to the extent that it is, dispose us to gaze at it in wonder, whether because it is intelligible or just because it is at all. More striking than this, though, is that there are diverse ways of contemplating reality that can comport with any contemplative act, regardless of level.[84] And for the reader of Aquinas, it is nothing if not surprising that the angelic doctor says nothing at all about the modes. All the more reason, then, to find out about them. The first is *dilatio mentis*, the enlarging of the mind, which takes place by pursuing exercises of attention and concentration. I can expand my mind simply by considering a leaf when I rest on a mountain trail. *Sublevatio mentis*, the raising of the mind, is a way of gazing in which one's knowledge is increased, whether by adding to what one already knows, by adding to what any

---

84  On the three modes, see Jean Châtillon, "Les trois modes de la contemplation selon Richard de Saint-Victor," *Bulletin de littérature ecclésiastique*, 41 (1940), 3-26.

individual can know, or by adding to what humanity can possibly know. In each case, and notably the third, the charism of prophecy, I must receive divine Grace in order to raise my mind to attain such knowledge; it is experiential, not discursive. Finally, with special Grace, I may approach God by way of *excessus mentis*, the overflowing of the mind, or ecstasy.

There are three moments in this third mode of contemplation. There is *magnitudo devotionis*, greatness of devotion, which happens when the soul longs to be taken out of the body and to be one with God; *magnitudo admirationis*, greatness of wonder, occurs with rapid insight into the heart of things; and *magnitudo exsultationis*, greatness of exultation, takes place when the divine light pierces the human mind and raises the understanding above its usual level so that it apprehends something of the divine. Dante's Aquinas values Richard's teaching as guiding us to be "more than man" [*più che viro*], and we can readily see what he means; if we follow Richard's teaching, we will be stretched. For one of the aims of *De arca mystica* is to cultivate

angelic wisdom in the contemplative soul.[85] If
we recoil at the very idea of being changed
into angels, we might wish to remember that
for Aquinas human beings resemble angels in
our intellect, even though our intelligence is
discursive, which must be corrected, insofar as
it can, by the practice of simple intuition in
contemplation.[86] Also, we may value Richard's
teaching for showing us how to be human as
such, the dignity of which surely involves
seeking to enlarge the mind and raise it to
higher things by attending to what is around
us.[87] Contemplation, for Richard, a canon regular, is part and parcel of the mixed life, a life
encompassing the gifts of Leah and Rachel,
Martha and Mary; if Aquinas differs from him

85  See Steven Chase, *Angelic Wisdom: The Cherubim
    and the Grace of Contemplation in Richard of St.
    Victor* (Notre Dame: University of Notre Dame
    Press, 1995), esp. 116-19.

86  See Aquinas, *ST*, 2a2æ q. 180 art. 6 ad 2.

87  Kant develops the same idea of stretching one-
    self above the common lot in a quite different
    manner, with respect to the *sensus communis*.
    See his *The Critique of Judgment*, trans. James
    Creed Meredith (Oxford: Clarendon Press,
    1952), § 40.

it is not because he prefers something other than the mixed life but because of an emphasis that comes with him being a friar of the Order of Preachers. For him, the mixed life turns on prayer and preaching — *Contemplare et contemplate aliis tradere* ("Contemplate and pass on to others what has been contemplated"), as the Dominican maxim has it — not on the more variegated life of a canon regular.[88]

We might reflect that Aquinas's strict separation of the active and contemplative lives, even though he advocates the mixed life, does not encourage him to affirm the modes that Richard proposes. For the modes cut across any distinction (including that between way of life and ecclesial state

88  See Aquinas, *ST*, 2a2æ q.188 art. 6 *responsio*. For his view of canons regular, see *ST*, 2a2æ q.189 art. 8 ad 2. Also see Gregory the Great, *MJ*, 27.24.44. Further, see Caroline Walker Bynum, "The Spirituality of Regular Canons in the Twelfth Century," in *Jesus as Mother: Studies in the Spirituality of the High Middle Ages* (Berkeley: University of Los Angeles Press, 1982), 22-58. The word "Dominican" begins to be used of friars in the Order of Preachers towards the end of the fifteenth century.

of life) between the active and the contemplative: anyone involved in the active life is free to contemplate anything and so can experience *dilatio mentis* or *sublevatio mentis* at any level. Unrestricted to particular levels of ascent, which Aquinas notionally assigns only to those in the contemplative state of life, the modes can be freely used in the world or in the cloister. Also, we might ponder that the levels and modes are not fitted only to the natural world as such. Human beings are created beings, after all, and reflection on our species, in general or in particular, is not ruled out as contributing to spiritual ascent. Nor is there any sense in Richard that the moral order of human life is overlooked in contemplation at any time, for human beings have intellectual and moral as well as physical qualities. (I will return to this point in a moment.) One question to keep in mind as we continue is whether Aquinas quietly assimilates the human order, physical, intellectual and moral, to the natural order when he consigns the natural order to secondary status with respect to divine ascent and, if he does, to what extent he does so, even when he affirms the value of the mixed life.

For those of us who live in the wake of the Second Vatican Council (1962-65), whose lives can seem mixed simply because we must respond to two contrary pulls — keeping oneself "unstained from the world" (Jas. 1: 27) and being in dialogue with it, as well as in far other ways — the idea of opening oneself to God by attending to the created order around us is certainly appealing. Perhaps part of the appeal is that we are already attuned, by dint of living after Shaftesbury, Kant and Schopenhauer, to aesthetic contemplation and our experience of viewing the natural world, whether beautiful or sublime, prepares us for untying the knot of selfhood before something far greater and more magnificent. (Another part of the appeal is our concern for the environment, which requires us to knot the self so that we can act in the environment's defense.) We will be attracted to approach God by way of natural beauty, only if we can be assured that it is convertible to being and truth. That would enable us to avoid aestheticizing the religious and lapsing into Romantic theology, on the one hand, and falling prey to a natural theology that has little or no need of Christ, on the other.[89] Another part of the allure is that in allowing ourselves to respond to God through wonder in creation we do not abandon our bodily selves but see there an excellence in having been created in just that way. Yet we also long for self-transcendence, not merely evacuation of self.

Transcendence, for Richard, occurs by way of the trained mind finding a higher level of immanence in its activities until it rests only in the triune God. The very exercise of attending to creation moves us, in and of itself, he thinks, to a more elevated condition and we reach in life the level to which God calls us. (Only later, with Counter-Reformation mystical theology, do we find the language of active and passive *contemplatio*,

89  On beauty as the "third transcendental," see Hans Urs von Balthasar, *The Glory of the Lord: A Theological Aesthetics*, 7 vols, 1: *Seeing the Form*, trans. Erasmo Leiva-Merikakis, ed. Joseph Fessio and John Riches (Edinburgh: T. and T. Clark, 1982), Foreword.

although an awareness of the marking is apparent much earlier, in Richard, among others.[90]) In Richard's exegesis of Exod. 25: 8-40, the soul ideally ascends in a steady manner, but it is not always so for other writers of his school, and that they have good reasons to complicate their model of the spiritual life. Achard of St. Victor (*d.* 1171), for example, figures ascent more surely by way of moral and spiritual advances than by close attention to the created order; for him, the soul undergoes fifteen transfigurations until it finally rests in the Trinity. He thinks that when it is conducted properly, the contemplative life has a descent and a pause as well as ascents: having achieved a contemplative state, one feels compassion for the poor, literally those with material needs as well as the neighbor as such, and seeks to serve them

90  See, for example, Theresa of Ávila, *The Way of Perfection*, ed. A. R. Waller (London: Dent, 1902), ch. 28. Infused contemplation was taken up as a theme by Réginald Garrigou-Lagrange in his *The Three Ages of the Interior Life: Prelude of Eternal Life*, trans. M. Timothea Doyle (St. Louis: B. Herder Book Co., 1947-48), 3, ch. 28, 31 and 32.

before resuming the life of interior prayer.[91] Achard also underlines the importance of the sacramental life in the ascent, something we can easily miss when reading Richard.[92] With all that duly acknowledged, let us return to Richard and to something admirable in his model of the contemplative life.

The idea of creation and Creator being in a vertical relation is a deeply held assumption of the ancient mind that ramifies endlessly throughout the twelfth and thirteenth centuries and far beyond. In one way or another, we find it in all the Victorines who write about the spiritual life. If we suspend the metaphor of vertical relation, however, we might be able to see something unusual and valuable in Richard. Unlike his confrères, he is concerned with an act as old as φιλοσοφία, namely a conversion of the gaze from without to within, which, for him, is passing from thinking to meditating until we reach contemplating in its several ways. It is

---

91   See Achard of St. Victor, "On the Transfiguration of the Lord," *Works,* 195-99.
92   Nonetheless, see *MA,* 2.7 and 3.15.

not simply philosophical, though, for Richard has learned from Hugh of St. Victor, *alter Augustinus*, that the eye has different modes. Hugh systematizes Augustine's reflections on vision in his commentary on Pseudo-Dionysius's *De coelesti hierarchia* in delineating three: flesh (*oculus carnis*), reason (*oculus rationis*), and understanding (*oculus contemplationis*), that is, perception, meditation, and contemplation.[93]

As already noted, Richard goes further than Hugh in his commentary in proposing four modes of vision: one used for ordinary sight and three used for successive grades of prophetic vision.[94] The second highest

93    See Augustine, *The Trinity*, 15.21-23, and Hugh of St. Victor, *On the Sacraments of the Christian Life*, trans. Roy J. Feferrari (1951; rpt. Eugene, OR: Wipf and Stock, 2007), 1.10.2. Also see Hugh of St. Victor, *Super Ierarchiam Dionisii*, ed. D. Poirel, CCCM 178 (Turnhout, Belgium: Brepols, 2015), 472. Hugh of St. Victor's way of presenting the threefold eye influenced Bonaventure. See his *Breviloquium*, 2.12.5.

94    Richard of St. Victor, *On the Apocalypse of John*, 1.1, in *Interpretation of Scripture: Theory*, 344-48. The text is dated to the 1150s. Richard's *De arca*

mode attends to the visual but sees a spiritual significance in what is before it (as in Moses viewing the burning bush); the third highest, *oculus cordis*, allows one to understand invisible things by figures or signs; and the highest mode, in which there is no mediation, is the contemplation of heavenly things. What we have as we ascend, then, are four modes of sight; one would pass from the one to the other until one can gaze upon the Trinity and experience no disparity between knowledge and love. There are many opportunities to experience *dilatio mentis*, *sublevatio mentis* and *excessus mentis* during the ascent, if one is well prepared and if God so wills. In the first four kinds of contemplation one almost never is lifted to ecstasy, which requires Grace; yet, even in these first stages of ascent, one may well undergo *dilatio mentis* and *sublevatio mentis*.[95]

*mystica* is dated to somewhere between 1153 and 1162. Richard points us to Pseudo-Dionysius, *De coelesti hierarchia*, 1.2.

95  See Richard of St. Victor, *MA*, 4.22.

*

There is a purification of the gaze in passing from perception and meditation to contemplation: not a transcendental purification, needless to say, but an ἄσκησις, for we have mostly lost the fourth mode of vision due to the Fall and must labor through hours of prayer, study and good works in order, albeit irregularly, to regain it and the tranquility at the base of the soul that characterizes it.[96] An Augustinian by intellectual inclination as well as by religious profession — he followed the *Regula sancti Augustini* — Richard is committed to the view pronounced in *De vera religione* (and drawn from Paul's notion of the ἔσω ἄνθρωπον) that truth abides in the "inner man," and so the mind's eye must be trained as much as the physical eye.[97] We

96  See Richard's commentary on Psalm 30, *Collected Works of Richard of St. Victor*, no pagination. Gregory the Great stressed the need for a calm mind as the ground of the contemplative life. See his *MJ*, 2.37.57.

97  See Rom. 7: 22-23, 2 Cor. 4: 16, and Eph. 3: 16. Also see Richard of St. Victor's treatise *De eruditione hominis interioris*, *PL*, 196, 1229-1366a.

can find that inner man only by converting our gaze by way of passing from what the schoolmen called *ratio inferior* to what they called *ratio superior*, from looking out to looking within, and thereby we gain *sapientia*, wisdom, not just *sententia* (thought) or *scientia* (knowledge). Husserl was attracted to the same text, which he quotes at the very end of the *Paris Lectures* (1929) and the *Cartesian Meditations* (1950), yet while Husserl took the "inner man" to be transcendental, Richard, like Augustine, sought an inner man who was created in order to transcend the world, a man whose soul was formed so that it would bear the *imago dei* and finally be one with God.[98]

Not that Richard stops with the gaze, for his allegory is also a coded naming of something like what, centuries later, Husserl would call the "regions of being" [*Regionen*

98  See Edmund Husserl, *The Paris Lectures*, trans. and intro. Peter Koestenhaum (Dordrecht: Kluwer, 1998), 39, and *Cartesian Meditations: An Introduction to Phenomenology*, trans. Dorion Cairns (The Hague: Martinus Nijhoff, 1977), § 64.

*des Seienden*]. For Husserl, these "regions" are not spatial areas but the highest generic unities that belong to an individual whole, each of which has a unique regional ontology that offers an eidetic science appropriate to it.[99] We can think of these transcendental idealities as marking out the ways in which phenomena can manifest themselves to us.[100] When they do, it is always within one or another intentional horizon, whether it be spatial, temporal, cultural, historical, religious, political, or something else. We approach a phenomenon with certain anticipations in mind: these constitute an "inner horizon." It is progressively filled as we gain intuitions of the phenomenon, while at the same time

99　See Husserl, *Ideas for a Pure Phenomenology and Phenomenological Philosophy*, 1: *General Introduction to Pure Phenomenology*, trans. Daniel O. Dahlstrom (Indianapolis: Hackett Pub. Co., 2014), § 17. Husserl describes regional ontologies in *Ideas*, 1, § 149 and formal ontologies in *Ideas*, 1, § 10.

100　See Husserl, *Ideas*, I, §§ 9-10. There one finds a brief, formal account of the regions of being, a doctrine that is quietly elaborated over the course of his career.

other anticipations prompt us to look further. Of course, we gaze at the object against the backdrop of other phenomena, which is known as the "outer horizon." Taken together, the two horizons mean that all spatiotemporal phenomena can never be wholly known; there is always another angle of vision to adopt, one that has not yet been retained by consciousness. Like Richard, but in a completely different way, Husserl thinks both vertically and horizontally. Yet there are no horizons that transcend the world, although, to be sure, they determine the sense of "world" and are not actually a part of what they limit.

Change though it did in some respects, Husserl's mature thought was always oriented by the motto *"Gegenstände im Wie"* ("objects in their way of appearing"), even when it was not oriented to spatiotemporal objects.[101] Not all phenomena appear in the same way. Right now, a number manifests

101 Husserl, *On the Phenomenology of the Consciousness of Internal Time (1893-1917)*, trans. John Barnett Brough (Dordrecht: Kluwer, 1991), 121.

itself to me in cognition, a pencil in acts of perception, my maternal grandfather in my efforts of recollection, and my holiday next summer by way of anticipation.[102] In his own manner, Richard knew this sort of thing as well, but in *De arca mystica* he tabulates the regions in a broader way than we moderns are used to seeing. Like Husserl, he addresses visible and invisible phenomena; unlike him, he attends also to divine transcendence, which greatly exceeds the transcendence of any *res* that can be led back to absolute consciousness.[103] For Husserl, there is no regional ontology of the divine.[104] For Richard, the Trinity is the horizon of all possible horizons, but it exceeds all possible

---

102 Of course, at another time, I might remember the number, anticipate picking up the pencil, perceive a photograph of my grandfather, and enjoy my holiday in the present moment.

103 See Husserl, *Ideas* 1, § 49.

104 See, however, Husserl's remarks on his hopes to discern God by phenomenological means in *Einleitung in die Philosophie. Vorlesungen 1916-1920*, ed. Hanne Jacobs, Husserliana Materialien, 9 (Dordrecht: Springer, 2012), 6.

experience that can be reported within the world.

Richard knew, in his own way, that givenness (here, divine *illuminatio*) falls outside the reach of intentionality, at least with respect to the highest levels of being. Trinitarian theology is unlike arithmetic, physics, the *ars memoriæ*, and the other sciences. Instead, following Augustine, Richard posits a fallen, albeit originally transcendent mind, which was made in the image and likeness of God and which, when convicted of sin and converted, can be reformed with God's help. To read *De arca mystica* today, in the wake of phenomenology, is to be struck by at least two things. First, there is the breadth of Richard's vision, which encompasses created things, both visible and invisible, as well as uncreated things that are invisible. Second, there is the care with which he poses the "how"-question, the many ways in which phenomena give themselves to us, in sensibility, reason, understanding, memory, phantasy, as affect, as broadening of the mind, as raising of the mind to higher things, as ecstasy, and so on — and the different capacities of the gaze itself: thinking, meditating, and contemplating, with three modes within the last group (and three moments in the highest of these).

For Husserl, the posing of the "how"-question involves a remodeling of how we usually think. Quite pre-theoretically, we all affirm the personalistic attitude, in which we regard one another as real, unique individuals living in complex social relations, all in a world that can be charted by maps and that is subject to time. Interlocked with this mindset is the natural attitude, a standpoint which philosophers might recognize as nicely described by Lockean metaphysics and non-philosophers will see as "common sense."[105] We change attitudes often, usually without noticing that we do, and Husserl commends one or two of them in particular, along with the importance of taking note of when we

105 See Husserl, *Ideas Pertaining to a Pure Phenomenology and to a Phenomenological Philosophy*, 2: *Studies in the Phenomenology of Constitution*, trans. Richard Rojcewicz and André Schuwer (Dordrecht: Kluwer Academic Publishers, 1989), § 62.

change them. For not all are of equal value, particularly when philosophy is the object. I will touch on only a couple of them.[106] For example, we can adopt the naturalistic attitude, which channels common sense into naturalism or physicalism, or we can go in the exact opposite direction, which scientists and humanists both take from time to time. One step along that path would be to embrace the theoretical attitude, which emerged among the ancient Greeks; in doing so, we would begin to conjecture about a phenomenon in such a way that we think of it by way of knowledge rather than practical use. This attitude is useful for the theologian, since it introduces abstraction or universalization into our reflections, and doubtless teachers in the twelfth century knew this when requiring their charges to study the quadrivium before embarking on theology.

106 For more detail on the different attitudes, see, for instance, Husserl, *Ideas*, 2, 10. More generally, for his view of attention, see his *Wahrnehmung und Aufmerksamkeit*, ed. Thomas Vongehr and Regula Giuliani (Dordrecht: Springer, 2004).

Had Husserl known of Richard, he would most likely have taken him to think and act mostly in the religious-mythical attitude, in which the world as a whole is expressed by way of μῦθος both in the sense that it is a set of beliefs in the world and that it occurs in a narrative which arranges those beliefs (or at least some of them) into a whole.[107] Thus used, the word does not imply "myth" in the usual modern sense. That meaning presumes a sharp divergence between myth and truth, in which an (ideally) unconditioned truth is yielded by the methods of the natural sciences. That sense would answer to the natural attitude or, more surely, to the naturalistic attitude. Richard's μῦθοι would come into focus for us as the highly

---

107 See Husserl, "The Vienna Lecture," *The Crisis of European Sciences and Transcendental Phenomenology: An Introduction to Phenomenological Philosophy* (Evanston: Northwestern University Press, 1970), 283-84, and *First Philosophy: Lectures 1923/24 and Related Texts from the Manuscripts (1920-1925),* ed. Sebastian Luft and Thane M. Naaberhaus, Husserliana vol. 14 (Dorderecht: Springer, 2019), Supplemental Texts, 8.

coded symbols, types of vision, kinds of wing, and so on, that we have noticed already; and for Husserl they would be ways in which Richard and his contemporaries could understand how the world, natural and supernatural, works. For us, however, Husserl endorsed a re-alignment to what he called the phenomenological attitude. To attain this attitude would be to suspend the existential thesis and attend only to how phenomena are intentionally given to consciousness (exactly as cognized, perceived, anticipated, recollected, fantasized, and so on). The act of attention would lead to imaginative variation that would allow us to give a satisfying description of the phenomenon without any adhesion of the psychological coloring of the individual philosopher. Philosophy would supply a firm ground for thought, one that does not rely on presuppositions. Also, it would sanction the contemplation of being, taken to mean the grasping of the intelligibility of phenomena; it would be directed to an intersubjective act of understanding rather than of criticism (Kant), struggle (Shestov), analysis (Russell) or reductionism (Quine), to name only some of the most familiar modern meta-philosophical positions.

It is worth noting that in his account of the many mental perspectives open to us, Husserl values the theoretical attitude precisely because it first allowed humankind to pass from θαυμάζειν to θεωρία, from wonder to cognitive reflection.[108] Even the shift to the phenomenological attitude is chiefly valuable in that it allows us to move from curiosity to understanding the intellectual structures of phenomena, which is another valency of θεωρία for him. We can see that Husserl prizes θεωρία in its philosophical roles and does not recognize it in its religious dimension, which is what chiefly engages Richard. For Husserl, philosophical contemplation occurs only in and through the suspension of all experiential interest, any practical intentionality, but Christian contemplation cannot do this, for the soul wishes to deepen a relationship initiated by God. It longs to attain final salvation for itself and

108  See Husserl, "The Vienna Lecture," 285.

others, although perhaps in its highest reach, in extreme sanctity, the soul can claim to enjoy the divine glory without any self-interest, even in a self that has been largely purified of sin. The philosopher seeks knowledge without presuppositions; the Christian must always lovingly presuppose a creating and redeeming God. To which we might add that the philosopher begins in wonder and hopes to end in understanding, while the person contemplating God begins in wonder and is moved to greater wonder (*magnitudo admirationis*).[109] There is no final understanding of

109 A longer analysis than is possible here would expand on what is said about wonder throughout this lecture. Genevieve Lloyd, for instance, rightly points out that wonder has the value of introducing a pause in a philosopher's quest for certainty. See her *Reclaiming Wonder: After the Sublime* (Edinburgh: Edinburgh University Press, 2018), 214. It has also been argued that a reintroduction of wonder, such as one finds in Heidegger, sharpens any distinction between the natural sciences and philosophy. See Mary-Jane Rubinstein, *Strange Wonder: The Closure of Metaphysics and the Opening of Awe* (New York: Columbia University Press, 2008). In Husserlian

God, not even for the cloistered monk or nun. The Augustinian line *Crede ut intelligas* works better with doctrine than with God himself, as Augustine himself knew very well.[110]

Nor does Husserl greatly value aesthetic θεωρία, although he admits that the artist's gaze is kin to the phenomenologist's. The artist cannot abstract himself or herself from an individual psychology, however, and is not single-mindedly oriented to the knowledge that is more secure than that afforded by the natural sciences.[111] So, once again, we can feel the old crevasse in the word

terms, one might restate the argument in terms of the naturalistic attitude rather than the natural sciences. A counter position, in favor of associating wonder and natural science, is proposed by Philip Fisher in his *Wonder, the Rainbow and the Aesthetics of Rare Experiences* (Cambridge, MA: Harvard University Press, 1998), 41. Finally, see Bynum's discussion of medieval wonder in her "Wonder," *The American Historical Review*, 102:1 (1997), 1-26.

110 See Augustine, *Sermons*, 52.6.16 and 117.3.5.

111 See Husserl, "Husserl an von Hofmannsthal (12. 1. 1907)," *Briefwechsel*, 10 vols, 7: *Wissenschaftlerkorrespondenz*, ed. Elisabeth Schuh-

"contemplation." It seems never to have fully closed and perhaps to have spread far and wide beneath our feet when no one was looking. One reason why Husserl thinks as he does is that, for him, reorientation to the phenomenological attitude is quite capable of securing the realm of the transcendent in the philosophical sense of the word (that which exceeds consciousness) but incapable of seizing the realm of the transcendent in the theological sense of the word (that which exceeds immanent or created being); its limits are those of mundane phenomena, whether spatiotemporal objects or ideal objects. We could attend to divine transcendence, he thinks, only if it were somehow always and already in the stream of absolute consciousness.[112] We cannot bring the deity there by means of a transcendentally purified gaze, and Husserl has no philosophy or theology of divine self-givenness.

mann and Karl Schuhmann (Boston: Kluwer, 1994), 135. See also Dorion Cairns, *Conversations with Husserl and Fink* (The Hague: Martinus Nijhoff, 1976), 59.

112  See Husserl, *Ideas*, 1, § 58 and § 51.

Of course, for Richard God is always and already in the human intellect as the *imago dei* according to which we have been made; it has been deformed, no doubt, because of the Fall and its consequences, but nonetheless identifies human beings as created in an exceptional way and to a particular end, the enjoyment of the beatific vision. By acts of ἄσκησις, performed in Grace, we can substantially reform the *imago dei* and so begin, in a preliminary way and only fitfully, to contemplate God here and now. That is possible, Richard thinks, because, with moral reformation and Grace, we come to love God more and more deeply. We might say that the Christian God can appear only in and through our intentional acts of love (ἀγάπη), which, although buoyed up by faith and hope and supported by virtuous acts, are still wholly incapable of making God give himself to us. Yet if we love him as the Gospel enjoins us to do, God freely gives himself to us in all manner of ways, as the Church teaches: in the sacraments, the fruits of the Holy Spirit, the infused virtues, the illuminations of Scripture, the beauty of Creation, and in prayer of all sorts. This self-giving cannot be reckoned by way of intuition in any sense of the word that Husserl would accept, although like many another before him Richard urges us to think of it in terms of taste (Ps. 34:8). If we are to speak of there being a divine presence, then, it must be done by an appeal to a non-theoretical sense, while the very idea of there being such an awareness must, outside exceptional circumstances, be firmly supported by public liturgy and private spiritual formation. One mostly points to divine presence, if one does at all, in retrospect, as one increases in zeal of souls. Or one sees it intellectually, as when kneeling at the Eucharist one recognizes that the structure of the faithful before the sacrament of the altar resembles the structure of the Kingdom. One kneels before Christ and together we represent the outer aspect of the Kingdom (while having it within), we are here (and still to come, even as Christians), and we come in weakness trusting in the strength of Christ.

If the God spoken of by Jesus appears only in and through love, we might ask if he also appears in love of neighbor and if this manifestation would be any different from the one just entertained. Now love of neighbor is more than civil pleasantness or even well-meant social work; it is ἀγάπη. Accordingly, love of God and neighbor are tightly tied together in the New Testament (Luke 10:27, 1 John 4:20 and Gal. 5:14, for example). "Neighbor" [πλησίον] needs to be distinguished from "brother" [ἀδελφός] or "sister" [ἀδελφή]. In the radical sense that Jesus gives to the word, exemplified most sharply in the parable of the Good Samaritan (Luke 10: 25-37), the neighbor is the person who breaches the horizon of one's world with a call for help to alleviate his material or spiritual poverty. He or she might be near or far, known or unknown. There is little or no question of liturgical setting here, although the efficacy of one's personal formation will impinge on how one acts. The person who has properly developed his or her virtues will not only feel compassion for the one in need but also act upon that prompt. In doing so, he or she shares the love that God already shows to him or her. If God manifests himself in this event, however, it will seldom be in the register of conscious experience. One can reflect only that, by one's own lights, one has acted as one should, but one gains neither theoretical confirmation of the goodness of one's act (it is almost impossible to isolate its effects in another person's life or to judge their value) nor much consolation from the deed (one might always have done more or acted better or from purer intentions). The neighbor might not be grateful or even polite in accepting help. He or she may even be an enemy and remain so. A divine manifestation is likely to occur only after the fact, as when reflecting that one's action has a trinitarian shape.[113] The love freely given by God to one and freely returned, however inadequately, to God is also shared with a third person, and this shared love deepens the love offered to God. The *imago dei* begins

---

113 Such is my sense of Aquinas's view that God must become the form of the intellect if he is to be known essentially. For Aquinas's own words, see *CT*, § 105 and *ST*, 2a2æ q. 175 art. 3 *responsio*.

to sing, but one can hear its music only in the understanding and then only faintly.

\*

I sometimes imagine finding a book, doubtless on one of my nighttime visits to the Library of Babel, entitled *A History of Non-Coincidence*. It would relate the discontinuous story of major distinctions. To read it would be to encounter the origin and development of the actual and the potential, deductive and inductive, *a priori* and *a posteriori*, necessary and contingent, absolute and relative, essence and existence, real and material (not to mention formal), analytic and synthetic, phenomenal and noumenal, absolute and modal, and so on. In some ways, it would be a fine textbook for undergraduates at the start of their philosophical studies. Having mastered it, they should be introduced to another book, found in the same Library, part of a long series entitled *How to Think*. Some of these volumes are on poetry; others are on painting; still others are on architecture, cooking, myth, exegesis, and ritual. I have never got to the end of the series, which snakes across several shelves, but I have skimmed the one on philosophy.

This last-mentioned book is a more demanding treatise than *A History of Non-Coincidence*, and a more illuminating one, as it indicates how and why distinctions are drawn, not just what they are once they have been set on the page. It considers contrasts between things, between concepts and between words; it presents divisions of rhetoric as well as of reason, expands on the diverse styles of making them, and the uses to which they are put, abstraction and definition being two of the main ones. The author directs our attention to the irreducible duality of Same and Other, as well as that of Like and Unlike. We are led to examine the metonymic and the metaphoric, and we learn to recognize all manner of difference; we see those that are genetic and those that are implicit; we see the descriptive and evaluative, the ostensive and persuasive, the abstract and concrete, the pragmatic, and many others. There is a chapter on separations caused by interruptions, one on articulation of conceptions, and a memorable one on the "wavy line" excision. We examine those distinctions that respect ordinary language, and others that, as Henry Sidgwick says, "clip the ragged edge of common usage."[114] As one reads the book, one gets the peculiar feeling of having become invisible, allowed freely to float back and forth in time, and able to look over the shoulders of Plato and Aristotle, Avicenna and Aquinas, Descartes and Kant; and one begins to develop a taste for philosophical idioms. After a while, one can recognize those who almost instinctively draw lines to get quickly to definitions, examples or counterexamples, and those who linger over these things by multiplying niceties of difference; one begins to discern those who clarify issues with one or two strokes and others who cloud the water with too much agitation. In an appendix, sundry diseases associated with division are described, among them, Scotus Syndrome (the condition of being attracted to distinctions no one else can see) and Husserl

114 Henry Sidgwick, *The Methods of Ethics* (London: Macmillan, 1874), 3.5.1.

Fever (the condition of being unable to stop multiplying distinctions).

If there is a book in the Library entitled *How Aquinas Draws Distinctions*, I have not yet seen it, although one would think the cataloguing system would place it near the series I have just mentioned. It is a volume I would very much like to read. There would be narrow discussion of the cut between the material and the formal, as well as the real, and examination of the different sorts of distinction of reason. We would surely learn that Aquinas had a rich lexicon for recognizing alterity and unlikeness, one that is apparent in the commentary on Peter Lombard's *Sententiæ* as well as in the *Summa contra Gentiles*, the commentary on Boethius's *De trinitate*, the volumes of *quæstiones disputatæ*, and the commentaries on Scripture and Aristotle.[115] As good a place as any to see this is, as one might imagine, his discussion of

---

115 See, in particular, *SCG*, 1.40 and 1.71 for Aquinas's remarks on God's knowledge of distinctions. On plurality, see his *Exposito super librum Boethii De trinitate*, q. 4 art. 1 and *CT*, § 72.

early misunderstandings of the Trinity in *Summa theologiæ*, 1a q. 31 art. 2, which is part of the tractate on God as triune. The question under consideration is "Whether the Son is other than the Father?"

In the *responsio* to 1a q. 31 art. 2 Aquinas first turns to Arius, and tells us that "we must shun the use of the terms diversity and difference in God, lest we take away the unity of essence" [*Ad evitandum igitur errorem Arii, vitare debemus in divinis nomen diversitatis et differentiae, ne tollatur unitas essentiae*]; then he adds "we may use the word 'distinction' because there is a relative opposition between Father and Son" [*possumus autem uti nomine distinctionis, propter oppositionem relativam*]. An orthodox theological treatise will always use "diversity" and "difference" in the sense of "distinction" [*Unde sicubi in aliqua Scriptura authentica diversitas vel differentia personarum invenitur, sumitur diversitas vel differentia pro distinctione*]; but an unorthodox work will use "difference" to mean distinction of form, which is mistaken because God is uniform. Yet because the divine essence is simple, the words "separation"

and "division" [*separationis et divisionis*] are
to be avoided; and because the triune persons are equal to one another, we should set
aside the word "disparity" [*disparitatis*]. And
because the divine persons are similar to one
another, we must recuse the words "alien"
and "discrepant" [*alieni et discrepantis*]. For
there is no dissimilarity in God. Turning to
Sabellius, whose heresy must also be side-
stepped, Aquinas tells us that we are not to
use the word "singularity" [*singularitas*] in
case we deny communicability to God,
whereas the word "only" [*unicum*] is also to
be bypassed, along with the word "solitary"
[*solitarii*]: the one may confuse the teaching
of the number of divine persons and the
other will deny the sociality of the triune
persons. Yet the word "other" [*alius*] may be
used appropriately, because the alterity of
the Son is to be understood as another sup-
positum of the divine nature.

"Distinction," as we generally use it,
mostly means "relative opposition" for
Aquinas; and while we see him cutting, slic-
ing, notching, and nipping the natural, supernatural and ecclesial orders in many

ways, so as to allow a concept to appear all the more surely (with new ones always coming towards us over the horizon), we often see him tracing a line in a particular manner. A difference is established, and the clarity that emerges has a complex ordered form. A line separates the contributive, dispositive or formative from the essential: and so a phenomenon appears. Thus, in the tractate on the active and contemplative lives Aquinas argues that the happy life, the *vita contemplativa*, belongs essentially to the intellect but that the movement to engage in that activity belongs to the will. Contemplation begins in the will, with a stirring of the love of God, and ends in delight, which is also in the will (2a2æ q. 180 art. 1 *responsio*).[116] The will does not supply the essence of the activity, yet without it in our fallen condition there could be no such act to have an essence. In a similar

116 Also see Aquinas, *ST*, 2a2æ q. 180 art. 7 ad 1. Aquinas points out that he draws from Aristotle in thinking of contemplation as involving the highest intellectual being and the stirring of the will. See his *Commentary on the Gospel of St. Matthew*, 5:10.

way, the moral virtues belong to the active life, not to the contemplative life; and yet without these virtues overcoming passion and disposing one to seek happiness, there could be no repose of our gaze on God (2a2æ q. 180 art. 2 *responsio*). A third example is found in the discussion of what we are to contemplate. "The ultimate fulfilment of the human intellect is divine truth; other truths enrich the intellect by their order to divine truth [*in ordine ad veritatem divinam*] (2a2æ q. 180 art. 4 ad 4). The remark is of consequence because it follows a reprise of Richard's six levels of ascent, each of which allows contemplation in one or another mode (although Aquinas does not mention the modes). Primarily, Aquinas says, contemplation is of divine truth, and secondarily of that which enables the ascent.

In one sense there is nothing objectionable here, for surely the aim of Christian life is the love of God "face to face," as Paul says (1 Cor. 13: 12). In spite of that, there is reason to pause and reflect on how the primary and secondary are arranged, for we might question the apparent division between "divine truth" and "other truths"; for is not all truth one? If we open *De veritate*, we will quickly be told that only the first truth, God, is eternal (q. 1 art. 5 *responsio*), and that every truth is from God (q. 1 art. 8 *responsio*). One difference between divine truth and other truths is that we usually come to know what is true of the deity only through what he has created, and we know created being only by way of *modus significandi*. The divine reality, *res significata*, cannot be fully known by us in this life.[117] We simply cannot grasp the manner in which God is. At issue is uncreated perfection as opposed to created being, especially fallen created being. Nonetheless, as Aquinas teaches, to the extent that something truly is, it is good. The question is what happens to fallen creatures like us who need to know the deity but who are not yet as we shall be.

117 That is, ordinary human beings cannot grasp the *res significata*. As part of his nuanced understanding of the modes of knowledge in Jesus, Aquinas maintains that Jesus enjoyed an infused knowledge of God. See *ST*, 3a q. 9 art. 3 *responsio*.

A light is cast on this issue in article seven of 2a2æ q. 180 where Aquinas considers what is involved in attaining the repose of contemplation. "Strife and struggle arising from the opposition of something outside ourselves prevent delight in that thing," he says, adding, quite reasonably, "because no one finds delight in that against which he struggles" (2a2æ q. 180 q. 7 ad 2). Finding support in Augustine's narrative of his spiritual journey, the *Confessiones*, he addresses the problem as follows: "There is no strife or struggle in contemplation by reason of the truth contemplated, though there is by reason of the weakness of our intellect and our corruptible body, which drags us down to lower things." The path to contemplation is pitted by the difficulty of reaching the *res significata* because of the fallen soul's diminished power of understanding, and the truths of created things can only prompt us along our way. All this is beautifully supported by Aquinas's theological epistemology in general, which turns on thought being subject to conversion to the phantasm; namely, in this life cognition must go by way of sensuous images produced by the imagination.[118] It is our human reliance on phantasms, as regards knowing the truth, that limits our earthly vision of the divine essence. In contemplation we seek to gaze upon divine reality in and through the phantasm and so we do not rely wholly on sensuous images but "upon the consideration of intelligible truth" [*in consideratione intelligibilis veritatis*] (2a2æ q. 180 art. 5 ad 2). We move a little closer to the angels.

A moment ago, I said that for Aquinas we *usually* come to know what is true of the deity only through what he has created. Is there an exception? In the tractate on prophecy in the *Summa theologiæ*, Aquinas considers what happens in extraordinary states of ecstasy, which of course are the highest events of the contemplative life, and which occur wholly through supernatural means. Ecstasy involves "a certain violence" [*violentiam quondam*] we are told. It is beyond the capacities of human nature, though not

118  See Aquinas, *SCG*, 2.77, *CT*, 1.83, *ST*, 1a q. 84 art. 7.

that nature as such, because we all bear the *imago dei* that draws us to God. One dimension of this violence is that in ecstasy we no longer understand truths "through the medium of sense-objects" (2a2æ q. 175 art. 1 *responsio*). Ecstasy essentially relates to our intellective powers, and only secondarily to our appetitive powers; with the body quietened, yet still joined to the soul, we can see into the divine essence. Only in rapture, *mors mystica*, is that possible (2a2æ q. 175 art. 4 *responsio*). Yet after rapture we cannot say exactly what happened or what was seen. To do so would require a shared experience that is expressed in similar ways by all parties.[119] When Paul was caught up into the heavens (2 Cor. 12: 2), there were "impressions" that remained in his soul, which enabled him to know what had happened, but he could not articulate the knowledge (2a2æ q. 175 art. 5 ad 3).

There is nothing in Aquinas, as I have just summarized a couple of his articles, with which Richard would demur as regards

119 See Robinson, *Definition*, 52.

contemplation, right down to *excessus mentis*
and the fuzziness of the division between consideration and contemplation. There is a difference between these two writers, though,
one that comes to light not in rapture but
when I examine a leaf. In doing so, I admire
its form, as Richard and Aquinas agree is right
and proper, and this admiration quietly
prompts me to ascend, in one way or another,
a little higher so that I might gaze upon God
insofar as I am able to do so.[120] Aquinas reminds us that only God is truly worth contemplating, and seems like Augustine to fear
the possibility of idolatry in gazing for too
long at nature, even though creation is good.
Richard, however, allows us time to take in
the created goodness of the leaf, to take pleasure in its color, its design, to appreciate the
part it plays in the natural world, and to prepare our hearts for God. The very insuffi-

120 Needless to say, Richard is not the sole me-
    dieval spiritual writer who regards nature in
    quite this way. See, for example, Ramón Lull,
    *Blanquerna*, trans. E. A. Peers, ed. Robert Irwin
    (1926; rpt. London: Dedalus, 1986), "The Art of
    Contemplation," 4.4.

ciency of the leaf, its distance from God, is part of the prompt to ascend. I can enlarge my mind as well as raise it to higher things. There is a suspension of interest in the leaf, since it cannot be put to use to any ends of my devising. But I do not simply seek to see through it but to see it as well, and in seeing it with attention I appreciate creation all the more. Is there anything else at issue?

\*

Both Richard and Aquinas take contemplation to be the soul's intense love of God, and in doing so they draw from the classical understanding of θεωρία while inflecting it in ways that had become traditional within the practice of the faith. Yet "love of God" has a double sense in Christianity, which we have already recalled in what Jesus tells us of the neighbor. The Great Commandment, attested in the triple tradition, names two commandments, going back to Deut. 6:5 and Lev. 19:18. It is given in Matt. 22: 35-40 and Luke 10: 27a, but the earliest version is most likely the one given in Mark 12: 28-31:

28. And one of the scribes came up and heard them disputing with one another, and seeing that he answered them well, asked him, "Which commandment is the first of all?"

29. Jesus answered, 'The first is, 'Hear, O Israel: The Lord our God is one;

30. And you shall love the Lord your God with all your heart, and with all your soul, and with all your mind, and with all your strength.'

31. The second is this, 'You shall love your neighbor [πλησίον] as yourself.' There is no other commandment greater than these."

Matthew varies the ending by saying "And a second is like it" [δευτέρα δὲ ὁμοία αὐτῇ] (Matt. 22: 39), while Luke has a lawyer say the words, simply adding to the first commandment "and your neighbor as your-self" [καὶ τὸν πλησίον σου ὡς σεαυτόν].[121] However the Great Commandment is phrased, though, it is evident that two obligations are imposed on Jews and Christians alike. The first of these can lead to freedom (the contemplation of God); the second points us to the perpetual constraint of having to answer the call of the neighbor.

One finds nothing specific in Richard's *De arca mystica* about love of neighbor, perhaps because it is so firmly marked in his vocation as a canon regular, which includes serving the poor and the sick, as well as having been addressed, if only indirectly, in *Benjamin minor.* Achard tells us that love of

---

121 Aquinas comments on the Great Commandment in his remarks on the version of it given in Matt. 22:39. For him, as for Augustine, we are to love the neighbor "either because he is just, or because he is becoming just," *Commentary on the Gospel of St. Matthew*, Matt. 22: 39. What we miss here is Jesus's love of the sinner even before he or she has turned to a life of virtue. The Good Samaritan presumably had no idea of whether the man he helped was just or unjust.

neighbor requires patience, whereas love of God presumes humility; and what could better generate patience than humility?[122] Their great predecessor, Hugh, commends us in a sermon to contemplate not only Christ's divinity but also his humanity, and presumably in doing so we would reflect on all of Jesus's responses to the afflicted who interrupted the horizon of his earthly life, at times even impeding even his preaching of the Kingdom.[123] Going back further, to the Augustinian roots of the spirituality of the Abbey of St. Victor, we might well cite Augustine himself on the importance of the love of neighbor, notably in his luminous homilies on 1 John.[124] In doing so, however,

---

122 See Achard of St. Victor, "[Second] Dedication for the Dedication of a Church," *Works*, 232.
123 See Hugh of St. Victor, "Go from your Land and your Kin," *Sermons for the Liturgical Year*, ed. Hugh Feiss, Victorine Texts in Translation, 8 (Turnhout, Belgium: Brepols, 2018), 95.
124 See Augustine, *Homilies on the First Epistle of John*, intro., trans. and notes Boniface Ramsey, The Works of Saint Augustine 1 / 14 (Hyde Park, NY: New City Press, 2008).

we would also have to acknowledge the many ways, subtle and not so subtle, in which Augustine, chiefly in his younger days, construes the relationship of the soul with God as overshadowing love of neighbor.[125] We should also keep in mind that Augustine commends us to love the neighbor for his or her virtues; the compassion for one who needs aid, regardless of his or her virtue, that one finds in Jesus is occluded. (We might begin by thinking of Mark 2: 9-12, Matt. 9: 20-22, 9:35, Luke 17: 12-16 and John 9: 6-7.) Richard, however, contemplates human beings as part of *rebus creatis*,

---

125 Certainly, the young Augustine is concerned, like the pagans before him, only with God and the soul, and the neighbor hardly appears. See *Soliloquia*, 1.1.5. Even thereafter, reference to the neighbor makes him or her seem somewhat secondary. See, for instance, *De vera religione*, 47.91. A fuller theology of the neighbor is slowly developed by Augustine in his later work. I explore this theme in my Étienne Gilson Lectures for 2020, delivered at the Institut Catholique de Paris, forthcoming as *L'image vulnérable: Sur l'image de Dieu en homme chez S. Augustin* (Paris: Presses Universitaires de France, 2020).

throughout the first four levels of ascent: what is good in Christian men and women helps us to rise to God who aids us, and what is wicked in those or other people reminds us of the need to rise.[126] (We might notice a tacit and partial convergence of Richard's levels and Achard's transfigurations here.) In this way, contemplation goes by way of the Kingdom as inaugurated here and now, and does not evade the struggles of ordinary life. That being said, let us see how Aquinas folds the commandment about loving the neighbor into his account of contemplation.

The figure of the neighbor first appears in the tractate on the active and contemplative lives in 2a2æ q. 181 ad 2 where Aquinas responds to an objection that the office of charity towards the neighbor [*proximum*], rather than acts of moral virtue, is the entrance to the active life. Against this, he urges that acts of all the moral virtues can serve to guide the neighbor towards the good by way of example; and, following

126  See, for instance, Richard, *MA*, 2.19, 2.22, 2.24.

Gregory the Great, he leagues such exemplary behavior with the active life. One might momentarily think, on reading this article, that the division between the active and contemplative lives almost excuses the contemplative from love of neighbor, that upon taking solemn vows such love is quietly folded into the love of God. Freedom in the ecclesial state of the cloistered monk or nun would be divided: there would be freedom from neighbor love so that one has total freedom to love God. As one might expect, though, Aquinas returns to the matter a little later, and gives the kind of complex ordering we have come to look for in his response to a challenging question. "The active life can be considered from two sides," he says, "and first, as regards attention to and practice of external works. In this sense it is evident that the active life impedes the contemplative, because it is impossible for anyone to be involved in external works and at the same time give himself to divine contemplation [*inquantum impossibile est quod aliquis simul occupetur circa exteriors actiones et divinae contemplationi vacet*]" (2a2æ q. 182

art 4 *responsio*).[127] This is true if one examines the ecclesial state of life in question: a cloistered monk cannot also be a mendicant, for instance. Only the eremitical Carthusians, who follow their own statutes, and who live far from secular communities, allow no guests, and a guest is a neighbor.[128] Yet even Carthusians must regard their brother monks and sister nuns as neighbors when they are in need, and prayer for the unmet

---

127 Of course, the division between active and contemplative lives continues outside the Church, sometimes according to somewhat different distinctions. See, for instance, Jennifer Summit and Blakey Vermeule, *Action versus Contemplation: Why an Ancient Debate Still Matters* (Chicago: University of Chicago Press, 2018). The distinction is folded into Marxism by way of "theory" and "practice." For a careful analysis of this distinction, see Jacques Derrida, *Theory and Practice*, trans. David Wills (Chicago: University of Chicago Press, 2019).

128 The Statutes of the Carthusian Order require canonical visitors to call upon their religious houses every two years; however, no Carthusian has any outside apostolate and receives no personal visits. Even correspondence with immediate family is regulated by the Prior.

neighbor is a part of all cloistered spirituality. Much depends on the weight one grants to the word "external" in the expression "external works."

Aquinas continues: "Secondly, [the active life] can be considered in so far as it regulates and directs the internal passions of the soul. In this respect the active life fosters the contemplative life, which is impeded by the disorder of the internal passions." This is no more than a recapitulation of an earlier remark in 2a2æ q. 180 art. 2 ad 1, that the moral virtues dispose one towards contemplation and aid one to complete it but are not of its essence. "In this respect," he says, "the love of God and neighbor is required for the contemplative life [*et secundum hoc dilectio Dei et proximi requiritur ad vitam contemplativam*]." Aquinas's deployment of one of his favorite types of distinction, the essential and the dispositive, jars somewhat here, as does the queasy sense that the neighbor is to be used in order to achieve the contemplative life. In preparation for his or her vocation, a monk or nun must love God, which is the very ground of love of neighbor, and that love is shown through appropriate exercise of the moral virtues. What happens, though, once one assumes the vocation of contemplative? For someone such as Peter Damian, who was required on obedience to leave the cloister, he has opportunities to attend to the neighbor, but are we to say that someone like Benedict would yield those opportunities when entering Monte Cassino?

Aquinas has already approached this question earlier in the *Summa theologiæ* when answering the question, "Whether the cardinal virtues are fittingly divided into 'political,' 'purgative,' 'perfect,' and 'exemplar' virtues?" (2a1æ q. 61 art. 5). The third objection runs: "In *De officiis* Cicero tells us that it is wicked for a man to say that he despises what most men admire, viz. power and office." His response is worth quoting in full:

> To desert from the human world
> and its just claims is wicked. Oth-
> erwise it is virtuous. Hence Cicero
> writes, a little earlier, *Perhaps one*
> *should make allowances for the lack of*
> *interest in public affairs on the part of*

*those who by reason of their excep-
tional talents have devoted themselves
to learning; as also for those who have
retired from public life because of fail-
ing health, or for some other yet
weightier motive, when such men
yielded to others the power and
renown of authority.* This agrees
with what Augustine says, *Love of
truth demands a hallowed leisure; the
demand of love undertakes fair busi-
ness, but if no one lays such a burden
upon us, we may devote ourselves to
the study and contemplation of truth;
if, however, the burden is imposed it
should be borne, because of the demand of charity.* [Quam sarcinam si
nullus imponit, percipiendae
atque inluendae vacandum est
veritati, si autem imponitur, sus-
cipienda est, propter caritatis ne-
cessitatem.]"[129]

---

129 Aquinas, *ST*, 1a2æ q. 61 art. 5 ad 3. The second
   quotation is from Augustine, *De civitate Dei*,
   19.19.

Accordingly, Peter Damian is required to perform acts of charity while Benedict is not, unless a circumstance impinges on him. In trying to understand Aquinas here much turns on the clause "If no one lays this burden on us" [*Quam sarcinam si nullus imponit*]. The implication is that the obligation to respond to the needs of the neighbor is a matter of ecclesial authority. But what of the authority of Christ? If we turn to Augustine, who is quoted here, we see that before he writes the sentence that Aquinas quotes in support of his position he tells us, "No one ought to be so completely at leisure that in his leisure he takes no thought for serving his neighbor, nor should anyone be so fully active that he makes no room for the contemplation of God."[130]

What causes unease is that Aquinas's distinction between the essential and the dispositive squares only awkwardly with

130 Augustine, *The City of God*, trans. William Babcock, notes Boniface Ramsey, The Works of Saint Augustine, 1/7 (Hyde Park, NY: New City Press, 20130, 19.19. The view is also pagan. See, for example, Seneca, *De otio*, 5.8.

the Great Commandment, and ecclesial authority is granted a higher status than the Commandment. In the case of contemplatives, love of neighbor seems to be wrapped by him into love of God, as formative and without further opportunity to be exercised; not even prayer for those "in the world" is mentioned, although it is perhaps assumed by dint of the liturgical life of the monk or nun. Also, we must remember that villages grew up around many monasteries in the middle ages. Cistercian communities, for example, were often far from self-sufficient and became sites of commerce as well as culture, and consequently there were many opportunities for monks to serve the neighbor, someone in the village or the someone who came to the village for purposes of trade. At any rate, it is sufficiently clear that, with regard to the ecclesial status of the contemplative life, Aquinas chiefly inherits from Aristotle (reward), not from Plato (obligation), even though as a friar of the Order of Preachers he inclines towards Plato's legacy. Now the motive of love of neighbor must stem from love of God, otherwise charity is no more than good manners and thoughtful social work. But there must be love of neighbor for this faith, hope and love to be salvific (Jas. 2: 14-26). More, we might say that if the *imago dei* is to be reformed, if we are to regain any likeness to God, no matter how faint, it is to be achieved by both love of God and love of created beings. God is love, and contemplation is an act of love; but God is also the author of great deeds, and if we are to resemble him, albeit remotely, we must attempt in compassion some work for the neighbor, as well as engage in prayer and study.[131]

When we begin truly to read the parable of the Good Samaritan (Luke 10: 25-37), that

---

131 The view is of course quite common in the twelfth century. Consider, for instance, Hugh of Fouilloy in his allegory of the dove as contemplative: "It raises twin chicks, that is, the love of God and the love of neighbor. Whoever, therefore, has these traits, let him put on the wings of contemplation by which he may fly to heaven," Willene B. Clark, ed., *The Medieval Book of Birds: Hugh of Fouilloy's "Aviarium"* (Binghamton, NY: Medieval and Renaissance Texts and Studies, 1992), 137.

is, when we read it contemplatively, we realize that spiritually each of us is the one Jesus sees with compassion as his neighbor, that *Jesus* is the Good Samaritan (with all the torsion that this implies with respect to Jesus as a Jew). We realize that the true *templum* is the Kingdom, seen not in the sky but in the broken horizon in which the neighbor appears, a sinner just as we are ourselves, and that each of us must be the neighbor whom Jesus helps before we can be called to help the neighbor who comes before us in his or her distress, in his or her mortality, in his or her need of forgiveness. And so, we come to realize not only must we see ourselves as neighbors of Christ but that in turning to the neighbor each of us must also be *alter Christus*, that we must embrace our poverty, in whatever form it takes, before we can truly embrace the poverty of Christ abandoned on the Cross. I stand before the neighbor not with any virtue I can claim or because of any virtue he or she may have but merely because I happen to be there and I am needed to help someone in distress. In other words, contemplation must go to God, but if it is to be contemplation marked by Christian love it must continually go through the Kingdom in order to reach the King. There are as many paths through it as there are people called to Christ. Yet there is always a general structure, regardless of one's ecclesial state: one gains a measure of self-knowledge through interiority, which leads to humility; and this humility leads to patience with the neighbor. The love proper to God begins in humility; the love proper to the neighbor begins in patience, even if the patience is wholly absorbed in praying for a neighbor who never physically appears before one. Only in ecstasy, which presumably is granted only by divine favor, is one momentarily released from the demands of the neighbor, for then the soul is held aloft from the body, as in death. Even those blessed by the charism of ecstasy return to their bodies and to the duties of following the Great Commandment.

In our usual condition, whether we are cloistered or secular, there is no one attitude to adopt when attending in prayer to God, for God gives himself differently if we approach him as Beginning [*principium*], as Creator, as Judge, as Father, as Savior, as Love, and so on. God does not change, needless to say, but we always receive him according to our mode. As the Thomist hermeneutical principle has it: *quidquid recipitur ad modum recipientis recipitur* ("Whatever is received is received according to the mode of the receiver").[132] These approaches are informed by Scripture and, as such, elevate the natural capacities with which we were born. Condensing these various courses, and with a nod to Husserl, we might say that the proper orientation of the contemplative, whether vowed to a religious order or simply practicing a mode of prayer "in the world," is what we might call "the Kingdom attitude," in which we respond to a call not only to that which is interior to ourselves but also to that which is anterior to ourselves. This is Jesus's preaching of the Kingdom and, before that, the creation of the original

---

132 Cf. Aquinas, *ST*, 1a q. 75 art. 5 *responsio*. One might well take this principle to be phenomenological in orientation.

Kingdom of peace and love. [133] It seeks to overcome any artificial division between the King and the Kingdom, any undue spiritualization of the Kingdom, as well as the distinction between the primary and the secondary, as Aquinas formulates it with respect to the contemplative life.[134] That division is appropriate for rapture, but there is no reason to figure ecstasy as anything other than an extraordinary gift.

We can learn from Richard that all that has been created responds to our loving

133  For a discussion of what I call the "basilaic" (or Kingdom) attitude, see my *Kingdoms of God* (Bloomington: Indiana University Press, 2014), Part 3.

134  This is not to say that the King and the Kingdom are identical. One worships the King, not the Kingdom. Only when one figures the Kingdom by way of the King's virtues can the two be regarded as one. Presumably, this is what happens when Origen calls Christ αὐτοβασιλεία in his *Commentarium in Matthaeum*, 14.7 and when Lull exclaims, "Thy Kingdom, O Lord, is Thy very Essence and Thy personal properties, wherein are goodness, greatness, eternity, etc," *Blanquerna*, "The Art of Contemplation," 5.

contemplation, not in dragging it down to earthly values but instead encouraging one to rise, doubtless with effort at times, towards the Creator. Smooth, single-minded ascent to God as *principium* runs the risk of prizing an ecclesial commitment to a life of contemplation that is conceived as over and above the solemn words of the Great Commandment. That Aquinas was aware of this danger is evident from his affirmation of the mixed life. For him, preaching and teaching are the substance of love of neighbor. As he says, "it is better to give to others the things that are contemplated than simply to contemplate" (2a2æ q. 188 art. 6 *responsio*). I am less sure that the rich tradition of the contemplative orders of the Church can be positioned so neatly as secondary. We are not in a position to know just how much suffering is deflected from the earth by the prayers of enclosed monks and nuns, and it is hard to judge the extent to which we have been edified by the continuous example of their faith, hope, and love. Nor does it seem right to deny that the joy of rapture is the ultimate sign of divine favor, one usually given only to the greatest contemplatives. At the same time, I am wary of distinctions that essentially separate our concern for the world and its people from the adoration of the deity, for I find no such thing in Jesus. Christian freedom is never freedom from anything in the Gospel and is always more freedom to affirm what is in the Gospel. Contemplation itself must go by way of the Kingdom until the Kingdom is no more (1 Cor. 15: 24), even if the Kingdom is glimpsed by way of fraternal life and prayer for those of us, sinners all, "in the world" or in Purgatory. Otherwise, it risks being θεωρία without due attention to the words of Christ.

---

I would like to thank Alexandra Aidler and Constant Mews for their attentive readings of an earlier version of this lecture.

# Abbreviations:

Henry Denzinger
*Denz.*          *Enchiridion Symbolorum*

Thomas Aquinas
*CT*             *Compendium theologiæ*
*DV*           *De veritate*
*SCG*         *Summa contra gentiles*
*ST*            *Summa theologiæ*

Gregory the Great
*MJ*           *Moral Reflections on the Book of Job*

Richard of St. Victor
*MA*          *The Mystical Ark*